FUNDING THE CURE

FUNDING
THE
CURE

CHARITABLE GIVING TO HELP THE MICHAEL J. FOX
FOUNDATION FOR PARKINSON'S RESEARCH FIND
THE CURE FOR PARKINSON'S DISEASE

Martin M. Shenkman, CPA, MBA, PFS, JD

demos
HEALTH

Visit our Web site at www.demosmedpub.com

Library of Congress Cataloging-in-Publication Data
Shenkman, Martin M.
    Funding the cure : charitable giving to help the Michael J. Fox Foundation for Parkinson's Research Find the Cure for Parkinson's Disease / Martin M. Shenkman.
       p. cm.
    Includes index.
    ISBN 978-1-932603-90-3
    1. Parkinson's disease—Research—Charitable contributions. 2. Michael J. Fox Foundation for Parkinson's Research—Charitable contributions.   I. Title.
    RC382.S54 2010
    362.1968′33—dc22
                                                        2009033851

Special discounts on bulk quantities of Demos Medical Publishing books are available to corporations, professional associations, pharmaceutical companies, health care organizations, and other qualifying groups. For details, please contact:

    Special Sales Department
    Demos Medical Publishing
    11 W. 42nd Street, 15th Floor
    New York, NY 10036
    Phone: 800–532–8663 or 212–683–0072
    Fax: 212–941–7842
    E-mail: rsantana@demosmedpub.com

Made in the United States of America
09 10 11 12   5 4 3 2 1

In honor of Martin Cohen,
who continues to brave the battle with Parkinson's disease.

By Gloria Cohen, Steven Dena and Sofia Cohen, Stacy Cohen,
Martin and Patti Shenkman, Jack and Miriam Shenkman,
Arnold and Vicki Shenkman, and Elaine Beresh.

Contents

CONTENTS

CHAPTER 4: DIFFERENT ASSETS CAN BE USED TO HELP FUND THE CURE

CONTENTS

CHAPTER 5: MEET PERSONAL GOALS WHILE FUNDING THE CURE

CONTENTS

CHAPTER 7: WHAT YOU CAN DO NEXT

Foreword

S INCE ITS INCEPTION, The Michael J. Fox Foundation (MJFF) has pursued a single goal: finding a cure for Parkinson's disease. This philosophy is evident in every aspect of our work, from how we prioritize research funding and assess grant outcomes, to our deliberate decision to hold no endowment or excessive reserves. We have always understood that our capital's critical role is to push research forward *today* so that we can close our doors as quickly as possible—not to ensure a long-term future for our organization.

In our brief history, we have met countless generous people interested in forwarding our work through planned giving. And while our mission of putting ourselves out of business remains steadfast, we are highly attuned to the incredible potential of numerous planned giving vehicles to help us accelerate groundbreaking research in the short term while providing our donors with major tax and personal benefits.

In 2008 Andrew S. Grove, senior advisor to technology giant Intel (and the company's past president, chief executive officer and chairman) and a member of MJFF's Founders' Council, announced his intent to bequeath a portion of his estate, up to $40 million, to our Foundation. His gift established a society to honor those who support the Foundation through their wills or other planned gifts, strengthening our capacity to speed delivery of transformative treatments and a cure for Parkinson's disease.

MJFF has also had the good fortune to work with Martin Shenkman, a foremost authority on strategic planned giving. We are deeply grateful to Marty for his ongoing dedication to helping educate our donors on what planned giving is, highlighting its unique capability to create a triple-win for donors, the Foundation and the nearly five million Parkinson's patients worldwide.

Of course, profound thanks are also due to those who support the Foundation through planned giving. Their generosity and foresight are helping bring all of us closer to a world where Parkinson's is a thing of the past. Learn more at www.michaeljfox.org.

Katie Hood
Chief Executive Officer
The Michael J. Fox Foundation for Parkinson's Research

About the Author

MARTIN M. SHENKMAN, CPA, MBA, PFS, JD, is an attorney in Paramus, New Jersey, and New York City. His practice concentrates on estate planning and administration, tax planning, and corporate law.

Mr. Shenkman was included in *Worth Magazine*'s top 100 attorneys in 2007 and *CPA Magazine*'s top 50 IRS practitioners in 2008 and top 40 tax accountants in 2009 and was the recipient of the New Jersey Bar Association's Alfred C. Clapp Award in 2008.

He is a source for numerous financial publications, such as *Forbes* (including an article in the July 13, 2009, issue that mentions The Michael J. Fox Foundation and this book), the *Wall Street Journal*, *Fortune*, *Money*, and the *New York Times*. He has appeared on numerous television shows, including The Today Show, CNN, NBC Evening News, CNBC, MSNBC, and CNN-FN.

He has published 36 books and more than 700 articles. His recent books include *Estate Planning for People with Chronic Illness and Disabilities* (DemosHealth), *Estate and*

Related Planning During Economic Turmoil (AICPA), and *Life Cycle Planning for the CPA Practice* (AICPA).

He earned a BS in economics at the Wharton School, an MBA at the University of Michigan, and a law degree at Fordham University and is admitted to the bar in New York, New Jersey, and Washington, DC. He is a CPA in New Jersey, Michigan, and New York.

FUNDING THE CURE

CHAPTER ONE

WE ALL HAVE A CONNECTION TO PARKINSON'S DISEASE

I HAVE A CONNECTION to Parkinson's disease (PD), and if you're reading this book, it's likely you do as well. Your connection will be unique to you, as mine is to me. But whatever your connection to PD, hopefully this book will help you to find ways to address that connection and help you to accomplish financial and other goals and protect and benefit yourself or a loved one, all while benefiting The Michael J. Fox Foundation for Parkinson's Research (MJFF) and furthering the vital goal of ending PD and finding a cure. To find a cure, however, we need to *fund* the cure. This is the task at hand.

For those living with PD, the urgency to find new therapeutic treatments, enabling those therapeutics to cross the blood–brain barrier, addressing the cognitive and mood effects of PD, lessening the side effects of levodopa, and encouraging other results, is tremendous. The task is indeed great. The damage caused by PD changes lives. Parkinson's affects an estimated 500,000 to 1.5 million people in the United States and perhaps 5 million worldwide. Each year, 60,000 new cases of PD are diagnosed in the United States alone. Scientific advances in the diagnosis of PD may increase these figures substantially.

The complexity of the disease is daunting. No means yet exists to make a definitive diagnosis of PD. In fact, by the time the disease is diagnosed, considerable neuronal damage will have already occurred.

The challenges to ending PD are many. Our help in providing funds as donors and our help in guiding and encouraging others to make gifts and bequests to help finance research and other activities are essential to those affected by PD and to the millions more who love and care about them.

The goal of this book is a simple one: to inform you, the reader, of the myriad creative ways you can give support to the noble and important mission of the MJFF and its cause of eradicating PD. The more options that you understand for giving, for *Funding the Cure,* the easier it will be to identify ways to help. Whatever your connection to PD, whatever your economic resources or situation, there are techniques that can make helping easier, accomplish more of your personal goals, help a loved one with PD, and more.

PD Background

While most people reading this book will be intimately familiar with PD, many will not. The following is a brief overview of the disease. Understanding the implications of PD will help you, the reader, the prospective donor, and the professional advisers who will help to implement the relevant planning ideas in this book, in a manner that best supports a loved one living with PD.

Parkinson's disease is a chronic, progressive neurological disorder that can affect both physical and mental functioning. The symptoms of PD can vary greatly from person to person, and even within an individual (e.g., over time and from hour to hour in more advanced disease stages). Assumptions about any particular person living with PD symptoms or level of functioning without a specific understanding of the facts for that particular individual can prove to be quite inaccurate.

At the outset, PD can be managed with medications and lifestyle changes such that a person with the disease can live a relatively unaffected life for years, even decades. Parkinson's disease, however, is always a progressive illness. Symptoms will worsen over time. The symptoms are permanent and will continue. Since PD generally progresses over many years, there generally will be opportunity for the person living with the disease, as well as his or her loved ones, to reevaluate their feelings and wishes over time. Thus some of the ideas presented later in this book may resonate today, whereas others may resonate years from now.

The most common symptoms associated with PD and examples of how they may affect the estate-planning process are reviewed below. Although PD is considered a movement disorder characterized by physical symptoms, it also may affect emotions, behaviors, and thinking. Parkinson's disease is a progressive neurological disease. Some symptoms present early and worsen gradually, whereas other symptoms emerge only later in the illness. The rate at which PD progresses and the particular constellation of symptoms that present themselves vary quite a bit among those with the disease.

Physical Symptoms

The main physical symptoms of PD, present even early in the disease, include bradykinesia (slowed movement), rigidity, and tremors. Bradykinesia can make it difficult for people with the disease to begin, or continue, an action. Rigidity causes stiffness, mainly of the arms or legs. Tremors can be mild or severe, intermittent or constant, and most commonly affect the hands. These symptoms can have a significant impact on a person's ability to write or sign documents.

Many symptoms of PD can make communication difficult. For example, bradykinesia affects not only voluntary movements but also spontaneous ones. Normal hand gesturing is reduced, and the muscles of the facial expression are also affected (sometimes referred to as the *Parkinson's mask*). These symptoms reduce the nonverbal cues that are often critical to effective communication. Other symptoms of PD may include dysarthria (slurred speech) and hypophonia (very soft speech). This can make it difficult to understand what the person living with PD is saying and can be frustrating for the speaker and listener alike.

As the disease progresses, balance and walking also may be affected. In particular, some individuals will "freeze" while trying to walk through a doorway or when approaching a chair to sit down. Their legs simply will not do what they want them to do.

Motor fluctuations, which frequently develop after several years of treatment, can be severe in people with PD. They tend to be particularly problematic in young-onset PD. At first, PD medications work very well, and symptoms tend to be relatively constant throughout the day. However, as the disease progresses, people with PD may experience a "wearing off" of their medications and a return of their PD symptoms as they are approaching the time of their next dose.

Those living with the disease can experience periods of extremely poor mobility ("off" periods) and good mobility ("on" periods). "On" periods can be associated with excessive involuntary movements (dyskinesias). Dyskinesias can manifest as subtle wiggling movements or more severe flailing movements of the head, body, arms, or legs. Subtle movements might give people the appearance of being nervous or restless when, in fact, they are not. Severe dyskinesias can make performing some tasks very difficult. People with PD can transition from "off" to "on" and vice versa within minutes.

Mental Symptoms

Mental symptoms of PD can include emotional difficulties such as depression, anxiety, and apathy, as well as problems with cognition (thinking). Some individuals also may experience psychiatric side effects from medications used to treat PD, namely, psychosis (delusions or hallucinations) or confusion.

Parkinson's disease may affect cognition in the following ways:

- *Bradyphrenia* refers to a slowing down of the thought process. It is the mental correlate of bradykinesia (slowing of movement). It can take longer for person with PD to respond to a question, even when he or she understands it perfectly well.
- Even early on, many people have subtle cognitive difficulties that may affect their ability to concentrate, multitask, and plan effectively. These are sometimes referred to as *executive functions.*
- Older individuals and those with advancing disease appear to be at particular risk for cognitive problems. However, the cognitive impact of young-onset PD has not been the subject of substantial studies as yet.

- As the disease progresses, some people develop frank dementia and may be disoriented as to place, date, or time. They may lack judgment and be unable to make decisions effectively. However, for some people with the disease, the ability to make key decisions will never be completely undermined.

While only someone living with PD can truly understand what the disease is and how it manifests, even a brief glimpse of PD gleaned from the preceding discussion drives home the importance of *funding the cure.*

Six Degrees of Separation—My Connection to PD

About six years ago, on a long summer weekend at a B&B in Connecticut, I came across journalist Mort Kondracke's book, *Saving Milly: Love, Politics, and Parkinson's Disease,* in a local bookstore. I was drawn to the book—which beautifully documents Kondracke's devotion and love for his wife, Milly, and her difficult struggle with PD. I read through the book that weekend to try to understand the impact of PD. My brother-in-law had PD, and I wanted to better understand what he was going through, as well as what my sister, his caretaker and partner, was experiencing. They never talked about it much. Most people seem not to.

Shortly thereafter, I happened on an article about a book by Michael J. Fox called *Lucky Man.* Again, my curiosity was piqued. Why was someone with PD writing a book with the word *lucky* in the title? After reading *Saving Milly,* I honestly couldn't comprehend what could possibly be lucky about PD.

Then, three years ago, my wife was diagnosed with multiple sclerosis (MS). Diagnosis with a chronic disease came as a shock to both of us, and everyone deals with it differently. My wife cried for days. We immersed ourselves in books, scoured the Internet for articles, attended seminars, and consulted with experts.

After tending to the myriad medical and personal decisions and issues, estate planning came to mind as something to address. An MS diagnosis changes everything, just as a PD diagnosis does. I was surprised at how little had been written about the effects of MS, PD, or any other chronic illness on estate planning. The few generic planning references about special-needs trusts and immediate powers of attorney were too broad and simple to do much more than insult anyone with a chronic illness.

I began to research and write articles about the financial aspects of MS, PD, and Alzheimer's disease (AD). I covered investing, estate planning, and charitable giving for those with chronic illnesses. Soon I was writing a book on the topic for the National Multiple Sclerosis Society. The book, *Funding the Cure,* documents step-by-step approaches that anyone can take to help support people with MS through giving to the society.

I wanted to outline creative ways to give to different disease charities; it seemed selfish to address only MS. In the course of research, I came across The Michael J. Fox Foundation (MJFF). I called the Foundation to discuss its work and the idea of mentioning the Foundation in an article about charitable giving and chronic illness. I found MJFF exciting not only in its unique approach and mission but also in the passion of those involved in the organization. Few people or organizations are gutsy enough to step out of the box and try something new; even fewer exude such purposefulness and vibrancy. MJFF has the guts. The zeal and excitement of the organization are captivating and catching. A request to review The MJFF's gift policy was followed by consultations on charitable gift annuities and insurance and then requests for articles for the MJFF newsletter, "Accelerating the Cure." The combination of MJFF's laudable mission and zealous staff creates a Nike-like atmosphere of volunteering—"Just do it." When the idea of writing a book on PD led to the creation of a new edition of *Funding the Cure* specifically for PD, and when the publisher advised that the manuscript had to be completed in three weeks, any other organization would have said "Good try," and quit—not the folks at MJFF. Impediments or unreasonable deadlines are not barriers, just challenges. Such a dynamic is not only infectious but also why the Foundation will succeed in its mission.

Ninety million Americans are living with a chronic illness. On the path to much-needed cures, MJFF's revolutionary model for driving high-impact PD science—emphasizing translational research to transform early-stage discoveries into valid therapeutic targets—represents a new paradigm for accelerating better treatments for many chronic diseases and addressing other health issues.

MJFF is committed to a nimble and adaptive approach, simultaneously pursuing a broad portfolio of therapeutic approaches to PD and constantly raising its own bar for strategic thinking about how best to speed progress toward transformative treatments and a cure.

- By prioritizing high-risk, high-reward research projects, MJFF helps researchers compile data and establish outcomes that increase the odds of potential breakthroughs moving forward.
- By fostering open collaboration among often-siloed researchers—academic and industry scientists—MJFF assists the field in germinating creative new ideas that could lead to new therapies.
- By focusing on the development of critical research tools such as biomarkers and better preclinical models of PD, and forging new systems that make it feasible for researchers to share these resources, MJFF streamlines the pipeline for disease-modifying therapies.

MJFF is the first to point out that its model is unproven. But the researchers on the front lines of the search for a cure—MJFF's advisors, awardees, and task force members—have been quick to embrace the MJFF's commonsense approach to pushing their work forward toward pharmacy shelves and patients' hands faster. I don't think that I would be going too far to say that we all would stand to benefit if MJFF's novel approaches to curing PD were adopted more broadly, by its counterparts working to cure other diseases, and by directors of traditional research-funding pools.

A recent issue of "Accelerating the Cure," MJFF's biannual newsletter, featured the stories of PD patients in their own words—stories of grace, optimism, and courage in the face of the daily challenges posed by PD. Mike McConnell, diagnosed with PD about five years ago, wrote: "We're all going to come down with health problems eventually. At least now I know what I've got."

Those 90 million Americans living with a chronic health disorder of some sort amount to nearly one in three of us. As Mike McConnell aptly pointed out, we'll all eventually have some health issue, or someone we love will. There really are no degrees of separation.

And though MJFF pursues an exclusively research-focused mission, its activities have created tremendous awareness of PD and of chronic illness more broadly. We all need to help cure PD, not necessarily because we or our loved one has PD, but because we recognize that ultimately, none of us will remain unscathed by the toll of human illness. We must find a cure for PD—we must invest our hearts and minds fully in the pursuit of cures for all diseases— simply because it is the compassionate and human thing to do.

In writing this chapter, I dug out my copy of *Lucky Man*. I'd dog-eared two pages when I read it the first time. On page 224, Fox wrote: "You're only as sick as your secrets." And two pages later, "Take the action and let go of the results." I first read those words six years ago, long before my wife's MS diagnosis. I don't recall the context in which those words spoke to me then or why I marked the pages on which they appeared, but the messages of those words resonated with my wife and I when she bravely made the difficult decision to go public about her MS to build empathy and understanding. If a health issue causes you to really stop and smell the roses, to focus on matters of substance, to realize that giving back to others can be far more rewarding then just doing for yourself, and to live with purpose and passion, then in some unexpected way MS or PD may in fact be "lucky." We've come full circle back to reading a book on a long weekend at a B&B in Connecticut so many years ago.

Richard M. Cohen, in his book, *Strong at the Broken Places,* chronicles the lives of five people, each living with a devastating disease—amyotrophic lateral sclerosis, muscular dystrophy, non-Hodgkin's lymphoma, Crohn's disease, and manic depression. Each of their struggles, their resiliency and their humanity, are common threads to those living with disease. Their struggles, messages, and determination are the ties that bind us all.

As Bruce Springsteen sings, "Now you can't break the ties that bind." Whatever your connection to PD—however close or removed—the ties do bind us. Join me in supporting and advancing the cause and goals of The Michael J. Fox Foundation.

Funding the Cure

There are many ways to give to MJFF and help fund the cure for PD. You can encourage or guide others to give in scores of ways. This book does not focus on describing complex tax and legal methods of charitable giving; you undoubtedly have skilled advisers who can help you in those matters. This is a book about people. It's about you and the people you care about. Rather than exhorting you to give or to get others to give, I'll share with you some of the things that you can do, even in a tough economy. Different approaches may work for you or other prospective donors, but hopefully, the examples, ideas, and illustrations in this book will give you a better understanding of the many possibilities available. You don't have to limit yourself to a particular approach; there is usually no single "right" approach. The goal should be to develop a plan that meets your personal needs and objectives and the needs of your loved ones, while benefiting the MJFF and maximizing tax benefits for you.

This Book

Each of us has our own unique ways to help the MJFF in its mission. This book is another way I've endeavored to help fund the cure. While the primary goal of this book is to guide others in making significant gifts to MJFF, all royalties on this book have been pledged as a donation to the MJFF. Whatever special skills or abilities you have certainly can also be used to help. Whatever your personal situation and financial circumstances, there are ways for you to contribute and make a difference.

How This Book Is Organized

THREE KEYS: PEOPLE, ASSETS, AND GOALS

Each of the steps I've taken to help fund the cure and many, many more will be explained. For you, the first steps are as follows:

- Identify who it is you're trying to help. Chapter 3 focuses on the different people you can help in the process of *funding the cure.*
- Determine what resources and assets you have available for planning. Chapter 4 reviews how many different types of assets can be used to help *fund the cure.* If you have significant resources, there are many creative and tax-advantaged techniques that can accomplish a number of personal goals. But don't worry if you don't personally have the resources. By helping those you know or meet to identify planning ideas, you can indirectly help to *fund the cure.*
- Address other goals you have. Chapter 5 shows you how you can achieve various personal, family, or other goals while advancing research to find a cure for PD. Your goals may include planning for your retirement, helping a child with PD plan for her retirement, helping to pass a business onto your heirs, or providing for the education and medical costs of your grandchildren. All these and many more of your goals can be integrated with steps to help *fund the cure.*

TAXES

Taxes! Because our tax system is so complex and costly, few charitable gifts are made without planning to maximize the tax benefits. Given the magnitude of the current economic stimulus plans and bailouts, most tax professionals expect tax rates to rise in the future, especially when economic recovery eventually takes hold. Chapter 6 reviews many of the tax benefits you can achieve for income, gift, estate, and generation-skipping transfer (GST) tax. While it's impossible, without a crystal ball, to predict what tax changes may come, some suggestions of how potential changes might affect your current planning to support MJFF are noted. Because of the uncertainty of future tax changes, it is critical that you have your accountant, estate planner, and possibly other advisers review the details of any plan before you implement it.

GLOSSARY AND INDEX

Jargon abounds, so we've provided a glossary and index to help ease the way through the planning ideas. The goal of this book is to offer you a wealth of planning ideas, each of which can result in a charitable gift of some sort to help *fund the cure* for PD. This book will illustrate charitable planning in an understandable fashion for those living with PD, those who have a loved one with PD, and those invested in seeing a cure. The planning is different from standard tax, estate, and financial planning because dealing with PD, as you well know, changes everything. This book is not intended to be a treatise on charitable giving. Your personal accountant, attorney, financial planner, and other advisers—as well as the expert volunteers and staff of MJFF—can all help to guide you through the maze. If this book can give you and others practical ideas to begin helping fund the cure, though, we'll be a step closer to achieving our goals.

Chapter Summary

We all have a connection to PD. Whether you live with PD, have a friend or loved one affected by PD, or from the standpoint of compassion and concern wish to help the millions worldwide who face the many challenges of PD, we all have a connection to this disease. We all share a common goal. Our mutual connection should motivate us all to help *fund the cure* for PD. A plethora of ways are available in which you can

- Achieve many of your personal planning objectives
- Benefit yourself or a loved one who has PD
- Do so using whatever resources you have
- Obtain potentially significant tax benefits

This chapter has endeavored to encourage you to consider charitable planning to help fund the research efforts of MJFF—to help *fund the cure*. The following chapters will show you how.

CHAPTER TWO

CHARITABLE
GIVING
BASICS

T HIS CHAPTER INTRODUCES THE BASICS of charitable giving. Many approaches can be taken. Writing a check is but one method, although the simplest and most common. More complex approaches will enable you to tailor a charitable giving plan to meet more detailed and personal objectives.

The Michael J. Fox Foundation for Parkinson's Research (MJFF) is dedicated to finding better treatments and, ultimately, a cure for Parkinson's disease (PD) through carefully funded and monitored research efforts. MJFF has focused its efforts on raising current dollars to fund PD research. This contrasts sharply with the objective pursued by many charities that focus on building a reserve of funds for future use. This unique philosophy is consistent with MJFF's goal of curing PD so that it can go out of business. This goal is not inconsistent with the many planned or deferred giving opportunities that can move us toward the cure for PD. If MJFF is successful in achieving its goal, any funds remaining as a result of your pursuing these more sophisticated giving opportunities can be then directed toward other causes and organizations serving those living with PD or other charitable endeavors you support. Having to address excess funds that remain once a cure is found is the dream problem we all hope for.

Carefully planned gifts to any charity also can help the donor (whether it is you, a family member, or another) achieve important personal, income tax, estate tax, and other benefits. To understand the strategies in this book, this chapter provides an overview of the many ways charitable giving can be planned and understood. The purpose of this chapter is to help you think about charitable giving in broad and flexible terms, to understand some of the basic concepts and terminology, and to begin to set the framework for how you (or those you know) may specifically help to *fund the cure* using the techniques discussed in Chapters 3, 4, and 5. The more technical tax concepts are left for Chapter 6, which will be easier to understand once you've identified some of the planning ideas you wish to pursue (or, as an alternative, you can merely rely on your professional advisers and skip Chapter 6).

When You Can Give

Charitable donations can be made at any time that best meets your personal, tax, or other goals. The timing of a gift is considerably flexible. Even if a charitable gift won't be effective until some future date, it can still benefit charities immediately by encouraging others to give and by giving assurance of future funding. For example, if you have been providing a certain level of funding, but the economic conditions make it impractical or impossible to continue that funding today, you could commit to the same level of support, thereby encouraging others to do the same, but simply pay it over several years to make it more affordable. If economic circumstances are more secure in a year, you can resume your historic pattern of giving without deferrals. Confirming a future gift today ensures that that gift will occur. Waiting to make the gift in the future, without creating a contractual arrangement today, will be far less likely to result in a donation.

Contributions to *fund the cure* can be divided into four categories based on the timing of the donations. These time periods are important to understand because they affect the planning opportunities available to you and other prospective donors:

Inter-Vivos Contributions: You can give gifts to fund PD research while you are alive. These are called *inter-vivos gifts* or contributions. The simplest and most obvious inter-vivos gift is for you to write out a check. But many other types of inter-vivos contributions are possible. You can make gifts of appreciated assets while you are alive, for example, cherry-picking particular security holdings that have appreciated. You can structure a charitable gift using a charitable remainder trust, charitable lead trust, or other techniques. These more sophisticated techniques can enable you to accomplish goals that a mere cash contribution cannot, such as benefiting yourself or a loved one with PD or taking advantage of the current economic environment, interest rates, or tax law provisions, all while still helping to *fund the cure.*

Testamentary Contributions: You can plan gifts that will take effect only on your death. These are called *testamentary gifts* or contributions. The simplest and most obvious testamentary gift is to include a bequest to a charity in your will, revocable living trust (an inter-vivos trust in which the charitable beneficiary obtains the gift only on your death), or any other instrument taking effect on your death. There are many additional ways in which you can make a testamentary gift, as described below.

✪ EXAMPLE: Jane Harrison is concerned that she faces a significant estate tax, but she is reluctant to engage in aggressive gift planning to minimize that tax now because of both her concerns over the economy and the uncertainty of future changes in the estate tax. Jane's goal is to benefit her selected charities and her heirs but to preserve flexibility to modify her plan if significant new changes occur in her financial position or the estate tax. She can always change her will, as long as she remains competent, to reflect modifications or changes in her overall plan. So Jane bequeaths that portion of her estate that is not subject to federal estate tax ($3.5 million in 2009, but changes may occur as the country grapples with funding the costs of the bailout and stimulus packages) directly to her children. Jane makes a bequest of a significant portion of her remaining assets under her will in a manner that is structured as a *charitable lead trust* (CLT). Jane's will bequeaths assets to a trust that will provide designated charities with cash payments for 20 years; after that time, the remaining assets will benefit her designated heirs. Because they will receive $3.5 million on Jane's death and the balance 20 years later, Jane views the deferral of the children's bequest positively as akin to a forced savings or retirement plan for them. The 20-year charitable income interest (actually an annuity payment) could eliminate any estate tax on the bequest (see Chapters 3 through 6). Because this type of trust will become effective only on her death, it is referred to as a *testamentary trust*.

A gift made while you are alive may benefit the charitable recipient more quickly than a testamentary gift. But consider that gifts made following death can open up opportunities for many new giving opportunities and new donors under circumstances that gifts made during your lifetime cannot. For example, if you were diagnosed with PD and want to make a contribution to help *fund the cure,* you might be wary of dissipating current resources until you have a better handle on your postdiagnosis financial picture. However, you might be quite willing to make a testamentary commitment with the hope of making additional gifts while you are alive when you feel financially secure doing so. The following illustrates a sample clause you could include in your will to benefit the charity of your choice with an unrestricted gift:

> *I direct my Executor to distribute and pay over to the _____ [insert name of the charity], with its principal offices in _____ [insert city, state, and zip], _____ [insert amount in words] $_____ [insert amount in numbers], for its general use and purposes.*

The following illustrates a sample clause you could include in your will to benefit MJFF with an unrestricted gift:

> *I direct my Executor to distribute and pay over to The Michael J. Fox Foundation for Parkinson's Research, with its principal offices in New York City,*

New York, _____ [insert amount in words] $_____ [insert amount in numbers], for its general use and purposes.

Current Contributions: You can give a gift that takes effect immediately. Such a gift is called a *current gift* or contribution. The simplest and most obvious current gift is for you to write out a check. You also can donate property (e.g., appreciated stock) to any charity today as a current gift. Charitable remainder trusts and charitable lead trusts are not current gifts because the designated charity receives the actual benefit only at some future date. Current gifts help immediately to fund the charitable objectives you have. *Unrestricted* current gifts permit the recipient charity to use the funds for any purposes it deems most important and pressing. In contrast, a *restricted* gift is one in which you mandate the uses to which the charity can put the funds. While many charities welcome and encourage restricted gifts, for example, a gift to provide counseling services for families of those with PD, MJFF prefers unrestricted gifts so that it can direct funds toward areas of PD research that it believes to be most promising.

Deferred Contributions: You can give a gift that takes effect only at some future date. These are called *future* or *deferred gifts* or contributions. The simplest and most obvious deferred gift is for you to include a bequest to a designated charity in your will. You could make a commitment to pay off a bequest over several years, which would be considered a deferred gift (e.g., pledge $10,000 as a total gift to be paid $5,000 per year, starting next year).

You can make deferred gifts using any type of trust that will make a distribution to a designated charity at some future date. A *charitable remainder trust* provides for a gift to the charity that takes effect in the future (e.g., when both you and your spouse die) and is an example of a trust that creates a deferred contribution. These more sophisticated techniques can enable you to accomplish goals that a mere cash contribution cannot, such as benefiting yourself or a loved one with PD while still helping to *fund the cure*. Deferred gifts are also referred to as *planned gifts* because you have to plan their payment. Although dollars from deferred gifts cannot currently help to fund new therapies and a cure, they can help immediately to encourage others to make contributions. Deferred gifts also can open many opportunities for gifts that could not be made on a current basis. Thus deferred gifts, over time, can help your chosen charity to raise new additional dollars to help its causes.

Combination Contributions: You can make a contribution to charity that meets all the preceding timing criteria. To help understand the relationship of the timing of gifts, bear in mind that all "current" or "present" gifts are inter-vivos (lifetime) gifts, but "future gifts" can be either inter-vivos or testamentary (at death). Some gift plans can include elements of inter-vivos, testamentary, current, and deferred methods. Although this might sound complicated, it can actually be quite simple, and it allows you to provide tremendous and flexible benefit to your selected charities, including the certainty that the organization can plan future expenditures (e.g., when budgeting for a particular program).

How Long Is Your Donation Effective: Perpetual Gifts

Annual gifts are the financial foundations of most charities. Annual gifts provide the funding, year to year, to continue essential programs and services, as well as to cover the administrative costs of operating most charities. However, although annual gifts are vital and will clearly contribute to *funding the cure,* each year professional staff or volunteers must again raise those same dollars to continue programs funded in the prior year. For donors who are willing and able, there is a better way. And if you're willing, there are many creative ways to become "able" to do it in a better way. What is that better way? You could *endow* (make permanent) your annual contribution.

⊛ EXAMPLE: Jane Brody's daughter, Susan Brody, was diagnosed with young-onset PD. When Jane first learned of her daughter's diagnosis, she made a donation of $25,000 to fund research aimed at finding a cure for PD. Jane has continued to make an annual $25,000 donation. Jane views this as just another way to show her daughter support and encouragement. Jane is in relative good health and just turned 70. Jane knows that when she dies, her $25,000 annual donations will cease. For her daughter's sake, Jane would like to have her annual donations to various charities serving those living with PD continue into the future, but she doesn't want to offend her son, who is less supportive of her daughter's situation. Jane decides against making a bequest in her will to perpetuate (endow) her annual gift because it will be so visible to her son. Jane fears doing so would only upset him and thus lessen the likelihood of him ever stepping up to the plate to help his sister. Instead, Jane opts to purchase a life insurance policy to be owned by each of the charities she wishes to benefit and payable to each organization on her death. In this way, for an additional annual gift (i.e., Jane's $25,000 annual gift, which she will continue, and the cost of an annual insurance premium, which she will donate as well), Jane can ensure that her annual gift will continue forever.

Endowing your annual contribution is one of the most important and powerful steps you can take to help any charity achieve its mission. Endowments, especially in economically challenging times, are a permanent and loud vote of confidence that resonates with other potential donors. However, some care must be taken in endowing your annual gift. How should you plan and structure the perpetuation of your annual gift? How can your chosen charities practically administer an endowment that is to last for years? Many donors haven't really thought through the implications of a perpetual gift. For example, the famous Barnes Foundation was created in 1922 and now owns an art collection valued at approximately $6 billion. The original goal of the foundation was to maintain and display the art collection at a house in Marion, Pennsylvania. However, in 2004, a judge expanded the number of trustees for the foundation and authorized them to build a more traditional museum in downtown Philadelphia because the foundation was no longer viable in its original structure. How do you plan a gift that will last in perpetuity in the manner that you, as donor, want to without creating undue problems for the charities? Use a written gift document that addresses many of the potential scenarios that might occur and how your endowment should be handled if a particular option occurs.

- If you name a particular family member to designate how each year's contribution should be used, what if that family member can no longer serve in that capacity? Who is the successor? What if that successor dies? You must establish a workable protocol to make sure that decision-making positions are always staffed.
- Include a detailed alternative "Plan B" and even "Plan C" because over time a gift may become impractical, things change, and you'll never anticipate them all. Focus on flexibility. If one of the charities you name is MJFF, in light of its mission to cure PD and then cease to exist, the donor agreement should provide that when MJFF achieves its goal, the proceeds of the insurance policy will be paid to other charities (for example, charities researching cures for other neurological diseases).
- Set a minimum amount at which, if your fund declines in value to that level, the monies will be distributed and the fund terminated. Below some specified amount (which will vary depending on your objectives for the fund), it is simply not practical to expect a charity to administer the fund. Your goal is to help your chosen charities, not waste scarce resources

administering the small amount of dollars remaining in your depleted fund. That minimum threshold should probably be inflation indexed. Many pundits have predicted that significant inflation may occur in the coming years. If correct, the threshold you set in nominal dollars today may be impractically low in 10 years if it is not inflation adjusted.

⊛ EXAMPLE: Jane Brody purchased a $1 million life insurance policy on herself, to be owned by a specified charity and to benefit the organization for its general purposes. Jane feels, given the long time frame, the insurance gift should be put to whatever use the designated charity believes best at that future date because the uses that Jane selects today may not even be issues in the future. Jane and the charity signed a written agreement to establish the Susan Brody Research Fund. Jane has donated a significant sum each year to the charity and has directed that it be used to fund research efforts that Jane believes, after consultation with expert investigators recommended by the charity, will best advance the development of medications to help certain medical conditions that her daughter and tens of thousands of others with PD have. Jane anticipates that, on her death, her daughter Susan will assume responsibility for allocating the funds to be distributed. However, recognizing Susan's frailty and the potential for the development of cognitive issues, Jane names Susan's husband and several alternative persons to assume this responsibility. Hoping that this narrowly defined research and funding project will succeed, Jane provides in the written agreement with the charity that if this narrow purpose is no longer practical or necessary, the person named in the agreement can allocate the funds for any other research or programming efforts of the organization. Finally, being practical about administrative burdens, Jane provides in the agreement that if the balance in her fund ever declines to $50,000 or less, which figure will be increased by the increase in the general consumer price index for each year following the year of the agreement, all the remaining money will be donated outright to the designated charity for its general purposes, and the fund will be terminated. If the particular charity does not exist, Jane lists general charitable causes to which the named persons can donate the remaining funds.

Comprehensive Example of When and How You Can Give

The various times at which you can make a contribution can be illustrated using an example that also will show you how to tailor these different time periods to meet different objectives, as well as a few of the many options that might be available in such a plan. This example will be developed to illustrate the expansion of a simple donation into a more comprehensive and valuable donation that can achieve the goals of a particular donor while assuring that the charity designated by the donor receives vital support, including a perpetual endowment of the annual contribution.

❂ EXAMPLE 1: **Current Inter-Vivos Annual Gift:** Robert McDonald is a regular contributor to charities that raise funds and awareness for PD research. Annually, he contributes $10,000 to fund these efforts for PD. When Robert's sister was first diagnosed with PD, the family's involvement with Team Fox not only raised money for PD research, but also got his sister active with a community of local Team Fox volunteers that really boosted her spirits. He also remembers the encouragement and support the members of Team Fox provided to his sister at that difficult time. Robert wanted to help expand those fund-raising efforts. So his annual $10,000 gift is designated to fund Team Fox fund-raising programs, which might include development and purchase of fund-raising guides, stickers, banners, advertising for Team Fox events, and more. The donation is a *current* gift because he made a payment this year. This is also an *inter-vivos* gift because it is made while Robert is alive. The benefits to the particular charity from this gift are significant because that charity can fund the cost of an important program that would not have been expanded to the level it has without Robert's personal commitment, encouragement, and financial help. This is an important component in making a charitable gift: In many cases, the gift is not only the dollars that a particular donor gives but also the encouragement, ideas, and leadership to make a particular program happen. Robert, after sharing his sister's experience, had a personal interest in promoting the continuation and expansion of Team Fox's efforts for others.

✪ EXAMPLE 2: **Planned Gift:** Robert McDonald could do more to ensure that his goals are met. The programs he funds must be budgeted and approved every year, based on whether his donation is received. Robert did not focus on this reality when he originally planned the contribution, and he would prefer to give Team Fox the certainty of knowing that the annual gift will continue so that the team can plan accordingly in the future. Robert has always intended to fund this donation each year, so he gladly agreed to sign a *pledge agreement* committing to do so. Robert's gift has now become a *planned gift,* in that a plan exists to continue paying it. It is also now a *deferred gift* (as well as a current gift) because his pledge will be paid in future years as well. The advantage to the particular charity of knowing that the program will be funded for the foreseeable future is tremendous. Resources can be allocated appropriately, and uncertainty is removed. For Robert, knowing that Team Fox's programs will continue is a significant personal reward, well beyond the valuable income tax deduction he receives each year.

✪ EXAMPLE 3: **Simple Testamentary Bequest to Perpetuate an Annual Gift:** Robert McDonald could do more to ensure that his goals are met even further into the future. If Robert dies, his annual gifts will cease, and so might the efforts he has encouraged and supported financially. Although Robert never considered this, when approached by his sister, he was grateful when she pointed it out. Robert would like to ensure that when he dies, his gifts to the particular charity will continue. How can his regular $10,000 annual contribution continue? Robert wants to *perpetuate* his annual $10,000 gift to ensure that even after his death the charity will receive forever (in perpetuity) $10,000 each year to fund its activities (see the discussion of perpetual gifts below). Robert is concerned that if he doesn't perpetuate this particular annual gift, it might be difficult for the charity to replace his gift and continue the same level of support for Team Fox's fund-raising efforts for PD research, which he feels is so important. Robert can include the language below in his will to ensure that the $10,000 pledged amount will be paid to the charity forever. Because this latter component of the gift is made under Robert's will, it is referred a *testamentary gift*. Because this contribution will occur only at some future date, it is also referred to as a future or *deferred gift*. Since this gift is planned (in contrast to his $10,000 annual check), it is also called a *planned gift*. Robert decides that, if he can bequeath $166,667 to the charity for this program, the program should receive adequate funding in all future years. He based his decision on the assumption that the bequest of $166,667 reasonably should be able to earn 6% and pay the $10,000 annual contribution forever. If he assumed a lower return, the likelihood of the gift continuing in perpetuity would increase.

▶ **SAMPLE WILL CLAUSE:**

I, Robert McDonald, direct my Executor to distribute and pay over to the _____ [full legal name of charity], with its principal offices in _____ [name of city and state], tax identification number _____ [fill in charity's tax identification number], $166,667 and that a fund be established in my name at The Michael J. Fox Foundation for Parkinson's Research, the income of which shall be used toward the funding of Team Fox's efforts and events to raise funds and awareness for research for finding a cure for Parkinson's disease. I recognize that the need for this type of programming may change over time and therefore authorize the charity to redirect the income from this fund to reasonable alternative purposes if it deems advisable. No interest shall be paid on this pledge. If the charity has been subject to a change in name or merger into a successor organization serving substantially the same purposes, such organization shall be considered to exist, and the gift and bequest above shall not lapse. If The Michael J. Fox Foundation for Parkinson's Research ceases to exist, then any successor charity to *which it turns over its remaining fund and assets shall succeed to any remaining balance in this fund.*

✪ EXAMPLE 4: **Ensuring That the Endowment of the Annual Gift Keeps Pace With Inflation:** Robert McDonald consults his financial planner, who explains to him the impact of inflation on a perpetual gift and makes suggestions as to how Robert can better structure the bequest to ensure that his goals are carried out. The financial planner explains that because of inflation, a fixed $10,000 gift per year will diminish in purchasing power over the years, possibly reaching a point at which, in terms of current dollars, the Team Fox programs Robert wishes to perpetuate may not be able to be supported from the funds he plans to contribute. The financial planner recommends that several important changes be made to Robert's bequest. First, no more than 4% per year should be paid out of the fund Robert establishes. This should permit the principal amount to remain intact on an inflation-adjusted basis. Second, instead of paying a fixed dollar amount (such as 6% of the initial gift, as illustrated in the preceding example), a percentage of the fund should be paid each year. If the fund is $250,000 in its initial year, the 4% payment will be $10,000, as planned. If the fund grows to $260,000 in the second year, then 4% of $260,000, or $10,400, will be paid. This concept, Robert's financial planner explains, is referred to as a *unit-trust payment*. This likely will ensure that the programs Robert so cherishes will be able to continue in perpetuity despite the impact of inflation. This constitutes a true endowment. It requires a somewhat larger bequest initially and a somewhat more complex payout, but it will give far greater assurance of Robert's goals being achieved. If Robert wanted to quantify the likelihood of this revised endowment plan succeeding, he could have his financial planner simulate thousands of hypothetical investment/payment scenarios (Monte Carlo simulation) and actually determine the probability of achieving the goal of perpetual funding. While this might sound complex, many financial planners, wealth managers, and investment advisors are well equipped to perform this type of analysis and help to plan perpetual gifts for donors like Robert.

▶ SAMPLE WILL CLAUSE:

I, Robert McDonald, direct my Executor to distribute and pay over to The Michael J. Fox Foundation for Parkinson's disease, with its principal offices in New York City, New York, $250,000 and that a fund be established in my name, the distributions of which shall be used toward the funding of Team Fox's efforts at building fund-raising and *awareness for Parkinson's disease research. The distribution from this fund in each calendar year shall be Four Percent (4%) of the fair market value of this fund on January 1 of that calendar year (or, for the initial year, the fair market value of this fund on the first day of the receipt of assets by this fund). This distribution amount shall be payable once per year within Sixty (60) days of the valuation date. The distribution amount shall not be prorated for any partial year. I recognize that the need for this type of programming may change over time and therefore authorize the charity to redirect the income from this fund to reasonable alternative purposes if it deems advisable. No interest shall be paid on this pledge. If the named charity becomes subject to a change in name or merger into a successor organization serving substantially the same purposes, such organization shall be considered to exist, and the gift and bequest above shall not lapse. If The Michael J. Fox Foundation for Parkinson's Research ceases to exist, then any successor charity to which it turns over its remaining fund and assets shall succeed to any remaining balance in this fund.*

⊘ EXAMPLE 4: **Starting to Fund a Perpetual Gift Today:** Robert McDonald consults his accountant, who suggests that he begin to contribute some money this year to create the fund to endow his annual gift in perpetuity. Robert's accountant explains that Robert can contribute appreciated stock to the charity to start the fund and obtain current income tax benefits (see Chapter 6). Robert's accountant also explains that although Robert currently faces a significant estate tax, it is possible that if the estate tax exclusion (the amount everyone can give away without any federal estate tax) is increased significantly, Robert's estate may not realize any estate tax benefit from the charitable contribution to the charity, so he might be better off making contributions when he has a highly appreciated stock to contribute. So Robert will establish the fund today, with a modest initial contribution. Each year, when Robert meets with his accountant to discuss year-end tax planning, they'll review Robert's portfolio and harvest stocks with large taxable gains to donate to Robert's fund. The accountant will coordinate the impact of this on Robert's investment allocation with Robert's financial planner. To implement this plan, one additional change must be made to Robert's will because now Robert's estate only needs to donate to his fund the shortfall between the $250,000 pledge to perpetually endow his annual gift and the actual dollars donated to this fund in prior years. This approach is necessary to build flexibility into Robert's will because it is uncertain when he will die and how much money will be in his fund from inter-vivos donations (gifts while he is alive). Although this planning adds a bit more complexity, it illustrates some of the many ways charitable giving can be coordinated with your overall planning and tailored to achieve specific goals. When you coordinate your charitable planning, income and estate tax planning, financial planning, and all your advisers involved in this process, significant benefits can be realized.

▶ SAMPLE WILL CLAUSE:

I, Robert McDonald, direct my Executor to distribute and pay over to the _____ [name of charity], with its principal offices in _____ [name of city and state], tax identification number _____ [fill in charity's tax identification number], the amount necessary so that the "Robert McDonald Fund" established November 22, 2010, has a balance as of the date of my death totaling $250,000 (inclusive of all prior donations to such fund, income accumulated on such find prior to my death, and this bequest under my Last Will and Testament). [The remainder of language could be identical to the prior example.]

What You Can Give

Too many donors and prospective donors believe that the only choice of contributions is cash, check, or credit card. Although every charity welcomes these types of cash donations, the opportunities to contribute are far broader. By carefully picking which assets you gift to a charity, you can maximize income and possibly other tax benefits and accomplish a host of personal goals as well. Detailed examples and discussions of each of the following items you can donate will be presented in Chapter 4.

Cash Contributions: Cash contributions, whether in the form of cash, a check, or a credit card payment, are simple to make (although, as illustrated earlier and throughout this book, even cash donations can take many sophisticated forms).

Tangible Property Contributions: You can donate tangible personal property, such as art, jewelry, or other property, to a charity. However, these types of donations raise practical, tax, and other issues. If you donate a grand piano, how will it be transported? Who will bear the cost of transport? Will it be used by the recipient charity for its charitable purposes, or will it simply be sold? Since the mission of MJFF is directed at funding PD research to find a cure, tangible property contributions would be sold so that the funds could be applied to research efforts. Since the mission of MJFF is so focused, the preference would be for donors to sell such assets and donate the proceeds. However, if feasible and necessary, MJFF may be able to accept tangible property donations or otherwise help you to identify a comparable avenue for achieving your charitable goals. The tax ramifications could be significant (see Chapter 6).

Intangible Property Contributions: Stocks, bonds, life insurance policies, and other intangible assets (contractual rights, in contrast to tangible property such as art or furniture) also can be donated. Some beneficial ways to do this were illustrated earlier in this chapter.

Real Property Contributions: Real estate often can be donated to a charity. This can provide tremendous tax and other benefits. You can make gifts of interests in your home, commercial real estate, and more (see Chapter 4).

Service Contributions: You may not have the financial wherewithal to contribute, but you always have a very important asset to contribute—yourself. Giving of your time, energy, and heart has and always will be the most important and inspirational contribution. It's far easier to write out a check than to donate your time to help an individual or group of people living with the challenges of PD or any other charitable purpose, or to see a project from its initial vision to reality. In fact, a tremendous way to contribute when you don't have the financial resources personally is to inspire and educate other potential donors who have the financial wherewithal to make significant financial donations such as those described in this book. Many prospective donors have a connection to PD and a desire to help but simply are not aware of the many options for gifting, especially how to give while simultaneously helping themselves or their loved ones. Many charities are in considerable need of volunteer time to run events, assist with administrative matters, and more. MJFF, because of its unique structure and narrowly targeted mission, provides a somewhat different opportunity. Team Fox members help to raise awareness and funds for PD research. Often for any charity, though, the biggest contribution you can make—and the primary goal of this book—is to alert those able to donate funds that there are creative ways to do so. Passing on the knowledge you glean from this book might just lead to the donations that *fund the cure.*

Who Can Give

Who can make a charitable contribution? Charitable gifts can be made by a number of different people or entities as a result of your efforts and planning. It can be far more flexible than just you writing out a check. By considering the various people and entities that can make donations for you, or because of your efforts, you can realize a host of additional benefits.

Donor with PD: Charitable gifts can be made directly by you, the donor. Your personal experiences with PD give you a unique perspective on how you might want to help the various charities serving those with PD and funding research efforts.

Family and Friends of Someone with PD: While someone with PD may not be in a position to make significant gifts because of the detrimental impact PD has had on his or her earnings and savings, loved ones may be in a position to give. These gifts can be used in many ways to directly (e.g., charitable lead trust) or indirectly (e.g., the charity providing services to those with PD expands those services, or a charity funding research into PD succeeds in finding a cure) benefit the family member or friend with PD.

Compassionate Donor: Some donors have no direct family or friends affected by PD but have become aware of the physical, cognitive, social, and financial consequences the disease can bring and, out of sheer benevolence, want to help to *fund the cure.* There are a multitude of ways this can be done, as discussed in Chapters 3 through 6, and many of these methods can be planned to generate income, gift, estate, or other tax benefits.

Agent: Every adult should sign a basic estate planning document called a *durable* (remains effective even if you are disabled) *power of attorney*. This document authorizes a person you name, your "agent," to handle your financial and legal affairs if you cannot do so yourself. When any prospective donor signs a power of attorney, the agent named in the power of attorney can be authorized to make charitable contributions on the donor's behalf. However, for this to be possible, the power of attorney legal document should expressly give the agent authority to make charitable contributions and indicate the scope of that authority. For example, the power of attorney could authorize the donor's agent to make gifts to charities that have historically received donations from you. The amounts that can be given also should be addressed. Donations may be limited to amounts that are not in excess of the maximum contributions made to the organization in any one of the three years preceding the donor's disability. If you have a specific charitable plan in place that requires actions in future years (e.g., you pledge $50,000 to be paid $10,000 per year), your power of attorney should expressly authorize your agent to carry out your plan. If it doesn't, then in the event of your disability, your plan may never be implemented because without express authorization, your agent may not be able to continue the donations. Some states, to minimize the risk of abuse of the elderly and infirm, have additional requirements for an agent to make gifts. You should discuss this with the attorney preparing your power of attorney.

If you have PD, you should have a comprehensive durable power of attorney that authorizes a named agent and several successors to handle a wide range of financial and legal matters for you. If you have a loved one with PD, you should be certain that you too have a durable power of attorney and that it expressly authorizes your agent to make payments for the care of your loved ones. If not, your agent may not be able to do so.

Trustee: The trustee under your revocable living trust could provide for the management of all your affairs as your PD progresses, including the right to make charitable gifts. However, similar to the issues noted in the context of an agent under your power of attorney, the trustee under your trust should expressly be authorized to make charitable gifts. If not, a question may arise as to whether the trustee is authorized to do so. If you create a charitable trust, the trustees will be authorized to make charitable gifts based on the terms of that trust.

> ✪ E X A M P L E : You establish a *charitable remainder trust* (CRT). A CRT is a special trust that requires a payment be made periodically, perhaps annually, to you for a set number of years or life. This payment can be made to you and your spouse (or in some instances, to other beneficiaries). So the trustee of the CRT could be required by the terms of the trust document to pay you and your husband a 7% annuity every year for your joint lives. If you contribute $1 million to this CRT, the trustee must pay $70,000 each year until the last of you dies. At that time, after any final payment due on the

$70,000 annual annuity, the entire balance of the trust must be distributed to the named charity as the charitable beneficiary. Your trustee is not only authorized, but he or she is required, to make this charitable distribution. Many CRTs reserve the right to you as the donor to change the listing of the charitable beneficiaries in your will. This is an optimal approach if you're planning a CRT for MJFF. When MJFF achieves its goal of helping find a cure for PD and closes its doors, you can always name new deserving charities of your choice in your will.

Designated Heirs: If you have a loved one living with PD, the uncertainty and difficulties PD creates might be offset in part by empowering that loved one to allocate the charitable gifts you make to a charity to fund specific projects he or she deems important. This element of control and involvement can itself be an important benefit you can bestow. You might do this in one of several ways:

- You could donate money or property to a specific charity and have these monies held in a separate fund under your name, to be used to fund various research or other projects in future years.
- A common charitable planning technique is for donors to establish *donor-advised funds*. In a typical donor-advised fund arrangement, you could donate appreciated stock before the end of the year to a major public charity and obtain a current income tax deduction

without designating the specific charities to receive contributions. In later years, you then can designate qualified charities, and your donor-advised fund could distribute money to the charities to be named.

- If you have sufficient resources and charitable intent, you could establish a *private foundation*. Your heirs could be designated as having authority on behalf of the foundation to make determinations concerning charitable distributions.

> ✹ E X A M P L E : Dorothy Harrington, as the donor, establishes a $100,000 charitable fund as part of a well-known investment firm's charitable gift fund (many major firms operate these to simplify donations). Dorothy and the fund enter into a written agreement governing the terms of how the fund will be used. The agreement provides that Dorothy's niece, Jennifer, who lives with young-onset PD, will direct the distribution of charitable contributions to the charities she chooses each year. While Dorothy anticipates that Jennifer likely will earmark each year's donations to fund PD research, she wants to leave these decisions to Jennifer.

Chapter Summary

Charitable giving can be far more flexible and dynamic than just writing out a check. You can give donations that are effective at many different times using a wide range of assets that can last for various durations and can even be directed by many different people. Your awareness of these options will help to open the door for you to identify many different ways that you or other prospective donors you know might be able to donate to support your favorite charitable causes while achieving important personal and tax goals and thus help to *fund the cure.*

CHAPTER THREE

HELPING PEOPLE YOU CARE ABOUT THROUGH CHARITABLE GIVING TO MJFF

PEOPLE OR CAUSES YOU CARE ABOUT are usually at the heart (literally) of most charitable giving. Because the tax rate is nowhere near 100%, you are always better off keeping your money or assets than giving them to charity. Therefore, even if tax breaks are important, you give to help a cause, goal, or person you are concerned about. This chapter explores how you can use charitable giving to benefit someone you care about and also benefit a particular charity. The person might be yourself, a loved one, a friend affected by Parkinson's disease (PD) or another health issue, or simply someone you want to benefit or protect.

Yourself

If you're living with the challenges of PD, a carefully crafted charitable plan can help you as well as your chosen charity. Charitable giving can benefit you in a host of ways. Consider the following:

First, Protect Yourself: The most important, and obvious, indirect benefit is that your charitable efforts help to underwrite the costs of research projects that may lead to discoveries of new therapies that will help you. You might wish, in light of the financial uncertainty of PD, to donate each year what you believe you can afford. You might simply harvest (select) your most appreciated investment positions each year and donate a portion of them to charity. This gives you the ultimate flexibility to determine what is appropriate to contribute each year, provides for substantial income tax benefits (see Chapter 6 for more details), and will give you the feeling of having taken action. Sometimes the simplest techniques are the most appropriate. In the meanwhile, the efforts and expenditures you might have put into more sophisticated charitable planning (such as those described below) can be channeled into ensuring that your assets are optimally organized and invested and that your estate planning documents are revised to best protect you against the potential trajectory your disease may take. When these essential steps are completed and you've had a few years to assimilate the consequences of your diagnosis, then you can revisit more comprehensive charitable planning.

Donate Appreciated Stocks: If you sell appreciated securities, you will pay a capital gains tax. You then have to invest and manage the proceeds. Instead, however, you could give your appreciated securities to charity in exchange for a *charitable gift annuity* (CGA). This CGA arrangement gives you a charitable contribution deduction (which will vary based on your age), and you will be entitled to receive an annuity for the rest of your life (or for the lives of both you and your spouse). This not only provides an income tax benefit, but it also eliminates your need to manage the assets. If you are dealing with the demands and stresses of life with PD, having a portion of your portfolio converted to a tax-advantaged annuity might be appropriate for you. However, unlike a commercial annuity, a charitable gift annuity has the important additional benefit of allowing you to know that you will be supporting a selected charity. You must be cautious about how much you commit to gift annuities because you cannot access the principal in the event of an emergency. Also, since CGAs are structured so that about 50% of the value ultimately will inure to the charity, you need to factor this into your budget and financial plan when making the decision. CGAs should not be viewed simply from the perspective of how high a rate a charity will pay. This is so because a charity that pays the highest rate may be taking undue financial risk to attract CGAs. Finally, even though caution and due diligence are in order before making any investment, including buying CGAs, the negative press about CGAs has stemmed largely from only a few charities and isn't necessarily reflective of CGAs generally. Be sure to review the appropriateness of CGAs with your financial adviser.

Consider a CRT: If you operate your own business or manage real estate property and it is getting more difficult for you as your disease progresses, or you simply feel that you need to reduce the stress that managing a business or property causes, consider donating the business or the real estate to a *charitable remainder trust* (CRT) and investing the proceeds, which could pay you a monthly annuity for life (or for your life and the life of another beneficiary or beneficiaries). This annuity may cover a significant portion or all of your living expenses. As with gift annuities, you must be cautious about how much you commit to a CRT because you cannot access the principal in the event of an emergency. Thus, in many CRT plans, a portion of the asset may be sold and a portion contributed to a CRT. On your death, the money remaining in the CRT will be given to the charities you name. You also can reserve the right in the CRT agreement to designate new charities in your will. Thus, if you name MJFF as the beneficiary of your CRT, and MJFF achieves its goal of finding a cure for PD and going out of business, you can then name new worthy charitable causes in your will to receive the funds remaining when the CRT ends. See Chapters 4 through 6 for a more detailed discussion, including ways you might wish to structure a CRT in light of recent economic conditions.

Implement a Revocable Living Trust: For anyone living with PD, establishing a revocable living trust to manage your assets, especially as disability progresses, is an important estate, financial, and personal planning step. If you do set up a trust to provide for the management of your assets, you should consider permitting some amount of charitable donations by your trustees, including the possible purchase of charitable gift annuities, if appropriate. This is important because if contributions and even gift annuities aren't specifically authorized, your trustee may be precluded from taking these steps or may be so concerned about violating his or her fiduciary duties as trustee that he or she might refrain from doing so even if not absolutely prohibited by law.

Spouse

Protecting Your Spouse and Benefiting Charity

If your spouse has PD, many planning opportunities are available that use charitable giving to benefit and protect your spouse while also benefiting charity. One of the key steps to protecting your spouse is the use of trusts to provide for the management of assets and other assistance before your spouse's condition warrants such help. *Trusts* are legal arrangements (contracts) in which assets are owned and managed by a trustee for the benefit of beneficiaries, such as your spouse. Trusts create a safety net that can enable your spouse to stay in substantial control of trust assets but have other persons as trustees or successor trustees poised to assist, if and when necessary. Using creative charitable planning, trusts can be created that protect your spouse, save estate taxes, obtain charitable contribution tax benefits, and benefit charitable causes that are important to you.

In many instances, you may wish only to consummate a charitable gift following the continued personal use of the assets (e.g., securities) or property (e.g., house) by your spouse. While you simply could wait and make the contribution at a future date, structuring the gift now locks in the planning results and, in some instances, may qualify for a current income tax charitable deduction. The contribution that occurs after a time of personal use is referred to as a *remainder interest* because it remains after the period of personal use. If your spouse is given the right to live in his or her home for life, and on his or her death, the home is given to charity, the organization is said to have a *remainder interest* in the house. Your spouse is said to have a *life estate* in the house.

Spouse Who Is Not a Citizen of the United States

Special rules apply if your spouse is not a citizen of the United States. In such a case, a special type of trust, a *qualified domestic trust* (QDOT), must be used to qualify for the gift or estate tax marital deduction. This means generally that when gifts or bequests are made to a spouse, they are not subject to tax. However, limitations and special rules apply if your spouse is not a citizen. The amount of gifts that can be made in any year without a gift tax cost is limited. If your spouse is not a citizen, you'll need to review these special rules with your tax adviser. If you establish a trust for your noncitizen spouse that meets the QDOT requirements, on the later death of your spouse, the remaining trust assets can be bequeathed to charities of your choice.

Charitable Remainder Trust to Benefit a Spouse

The *charitable remainder trust* (CRT) technique was introduced briefly in Chapter 2. The typical or "plain vanilla" use of a CRT is for you to donate appreciated property to the CRT, which sells the property without incurring capital gains. You receive an income tax charitable contribution deduction, and the CRT pays you an annual annuity for life. The CRT technique might be reasonable to use even if assets are not substantially appreciated because it still can provide important personal and other benefits. Have your tax adviser "run the numbers."

The "plain vanilla" CRT plan can be modified in different ways so that you can achieve the goal of protecting a spouse with PD and assuring him or her a cash flow for life, free of any responsibility to manage the assets. Each of the variations discussed below can also help you to accomplish important tax saving and charitable goals. In many cases, a combination of these techniques may provide the best result. In all situations, these techniques should be part of an overall estate and financial plan that addresses all your needs and goals, and these techniques should be used only for a portion of your wealth.

Marital Gift Followed by Spousal CRT: If you have assets, such as appreciated growth stock mutual funds, real estate, or investment limited-partnership interests, you can gift them to your spouse. Your spouse then can establish a CRT for his or her benefit and contribute the appreciated assets to the CRT. The CRT can continue the current investments as long as necessary and then, at the appropriate time, sell the assets and reinvest the proceeds, free of any capital gains tax, into income-oriented funds. For example, if you anticipate that economic recovery or future inflation will drive up asset values, this plan would fit those circumstances. The income from the CRT's revised asset-allocation strategy can be used to pay your spouse an annuity for life. He or she won't have to manage the assets and will be free from those pressures. An income tax charitable contribution deduction could be realized on your joint income tax return when the CRT is formed and the mutual funds contributed. When the CRT sells the assets, no capital gains tax should apply (and if tax rates rise, this benefit will increase). Your spouse can have an annuity payment made periodically for the rest of his or her life. On his or her death, a designated charity will receive the remaining assets held in the CRT. Importantly, that designated charity will realize a current intangible benefit from the date the CRT is formed, in that it will be able to announce the commitment in its efforts to engage other donors. During tough economic times, the confidence a large CRT can create among other potential donors can be especially significant.

Create a Joint Spousal CRT: Instead of giving assets to your spouse to fund a trust for him or her only, you might feel that you need some of the income (cash flow in the form of an annuity payment) for your future expenses (e.g., your retirement). Therefore, instead of having just your spouse set up the CRT, you can set up a CRT that pays a joint annuity payment to both of you for life. This will ensure you that if your spouse dies before you, you will continue to receive an annuity payment for life. Thus the annuity payment from the CRT to you and your spouse will continue for the longer of your life or the life of your spouse. There will be no estate tax on either your death or the death of your spouse. On your death, your estate will qualify for both a charitable contribution deduction and an estate tax marital deduction (for the interest your surviving spouse receives in the CRT). This ensures that no tax is assessed as a result of any interest you had in the CRT on death. Since the estate tax repeal efforts seemed to have waned in light of federal deficits, this approach could prove valuable in future years.

An illustration of a CRT will help you to understand how you can benefit your spouse and a charity using a CRT.

♢ EXAMPLE: Adam Grossman wants to provide for the protection of his wife, Elana, who lives with PD. Adam contemplates donating $1 million of stock that he has held for many years and that has appreciated substantially over its $150,000 purchase price. Because Adam has already engaged in considerable estate planning to benefit their children, he would like to benefit various charities that fund PD research following his and Elana's deaths. Adam is hopeful that setting up this type of future benefit for charities will encourage others to make major current and deferred gifts, thereby hastening the research that hopefully will help his wife. Adam decides to establish an inter-vivos (while he is alive) CRT for both himself and Elana. Both Adam and Elana will obtain current interests in the CRT. A current income tax deduction will be permitted, based on the present value of the future interest the charities will receive. A deduction is permitted because the rights of the charities are fixed in a manner that conforms to the tax law requirements for a current deduction. A specified payout must occur in each year (or monthly or quarterly, if required in the trust). No additional payments may be made to Adam or Elana, other than those fixed in the CRT document when it is established. Properly structured, this also will qualify for a gift tax marital deduction (because Adam is making a gift to Elana through the annuity payments she will receive for her life). However, should Elana face an emergency, the trustees cannot distribute the principal of the trust to her, so Adam has made sure that other resources are available to her in the event an emergency occurs. On the death of the last of Adam and Elana, the principal remaining in the trust is to be distributed to the designated charities to establish a research grant in their memory. The charities are remainder beneficiaries of the CRT. Adam and Elana reserve in the CRT document the right to name successor charities in the event future developments result in new charities better meeting their objectives in the future.

Combining Charitable and Marital Planning

Although the tax benefits of a CRT are substantial, there is a major drawback you must consider, especially if your spouse has PD. Once assets are contributed to the CRT, you cannot access the principal. The only right you and your spouse have is to receive the annuity payments as planned for in the trust agreement that creates the CRT. Thus, even if one of the CRT approaches described here is great for some of your wealth, it is unlikely to be appropriate for all your assets, and if your economic resources are limited, it may be inappropriate.

Another approach is to take advantage of both the charitable contribution deduction and the marital deduction. You could establish a commonly used *marital trust* to protect your spouse in your will (a *testamentary* bequest) or while you are alive (an *inter-vivos* marital trust). This trust can protect your spouse by providing professional management of the assets in the trust, trustees who can pay bills and handle other matters for your spouse if necessary, protection from lawsuits and claims, and other benefits. If your will establishes this commonly used trust for your spouse, no estate tax will be applicable on your death. If your spouse is a U.S. citizen, the most commonly used trust of this nature is called a *qualified terminable interest property* (QTIP) *trust* (or a QDOT if your spouse is not a citizen). This approach is not viable for a nonmarried partner (see the discussions below). The significant advantage of this trust over the CRT is that in an emergency, the trustees can invade the principal of the trust and use any or all of it for the care of your spouse. Then, following the death of your spouse, whatever assets remain in the QTIP trust can be contributed to charity. In tax parlance, the charity is the *remainder beneficiary* of this trust. While this approach is simpler and more flexible than the CRT, no income tax deduction is available with a QTIP trust with a charitable remainder, as there would be when a charitable remainder trust is used with you and your spouse named as income beneficiaries. In many cases, a combination of these techniques may present the best approach to protecting your spouse.

The following example illustrates how you, as a prospective donor, can accomplish the important personal goals of protecting your spouse who has PD and simultaneously creating a charitable plan to benefit PD-related causes (e.g., research, programs, advocacy, etc.).

⚙ EXAMPLE: Cindy Jones' husband Sam has young-onset PD. Cindy wants to provide protection for Sam for his life, but on his demise, Cindy wants to benefit charities that advocate for those with PD. Cindy establishes an inter-vivos (while she is alive) marital trust (QTIP trust) for Sam. Considering Sam's young age, the ability the QTIP trust permits to access principal in an emergency is essential, something the CRT approach would not allow. Sam has a current interest in the trust. No current income tax deduction is permitted for the future charitable gifts after Sam's death because the rights of the charity are not fixed in a manner that conforms to the tax law requirements for a current charitable deduction. To protect Sam, the trust may pay any necessary amounts of the trust principal (assets) to Sam or for his benefit during Sam's lifetime. An institutional trust company is named as cotrustee to serve with Sam. This ensures Sam's involvement in his own trust decisions and also ensures that if he can no longer fully participate in the management of the trust, the trust company will provide for whatever management and other services he needs. Properly structured, this trust will qualify for a gift tax marital deduction when Cindy establishes it. During Sam's lifetime, all income must be distributed at least annually. In addition, should Sam face an emergency, the trustees may distribute principal to him. On Sam's demise, the principal remaining in the trust is to be distributed to charities as the remainder beneficiaries. No current charitable contribution deduction will be realized. On Sam's death, although the value of the entire trust will be included in his taxable estate, an equal and offsetting charitable contribution deduction will be available.

Child

If you have a child diagnosed with PD, a number of steps are available for you to take to protect your child. The term *child* is used to describe your relationship to the person living with PD, not the age of your son or daughter, so this discussion will address PD as well as young-onset PD. Each of these steps also might be tailored to have a charitable connection. The following discussion reviews possibilities based on some of the estate planning documents you might use in your own planning.

Power of Attorney

This common estate planning document designates a person (agent) to manage your financial, legal, and other affairs if you cannot do so. The historical development of the power of attorney is such that if you have an adult child whom you are not obligated by law to support, your agent may not have the authority to expend funds for that child. If your child is living with PD, especially if he or she has young-onset PD that limits asset accumulation during a truncated work career, this could be financially devastating. For example, if your son was diagnosed with young-onset PD at age 40 and ceased working by age 47, he or she might have had the ability to accumulate significant savings, but not what he or she would have accumulated if he or she could have worked until age 65+ if he or she had not been impeded by PD. Therefore, it is vital that specific provisions be incorporated into your power of attorney that not only permit your agent to provide financial support to your child but also perhaps even direct him or her to do so. Any gifts in excess of the annual gift tax exclusion ($13,000 in 2009, but the amount is inflation indexed) will be subject to tax. Your agent also can make direct payments for medical or educational expenses without limit and without gift tax consequences. While you are tailoring your power of attorney to address assisting your child, give some consideration to having your lawyer modify the gift provisions to include the right to make charitable gifts and purchase *charitable gift annuities* (CGAs). If your child has young-onset PD and is receiving support under governmental needs tested programs, the gift powers should be limited to avoid jeopardizing your child's qualifications.

Revocable Living Trust

Many people use *revocable living trusts* to avoid probate, although a far more important use is to manage assets during illness or disability. If you have a revocable living trust as part of your estate plan, be sure to have your attorney make modifications similar to those described earlier for a power of attorney if your child has young-onset PD or PD.

Will

Your will should probably include a trust to protect your child/beneficiary who is living with PD. The trust can provide for the management of assets in the event your child has reached a point at which he or she cannot easily manage his or her own financial affairs. Whether this protection is required now or possibly at some time in the future, a trust tailored to protect your child while maintaining his or her involvement and dignity (perhaps as a cotrustee) is often the ideal solution. Review with the attorney drafting your will and trusts whether or not any trusts created should be *special needs trusts* (SNTs), depending on your child's age and financial and health status. As with all estate planning documents, your will can provide a wonderful way to tailor a charitable bequest.

    ✪ EXAMPLE: Jim Johnson has two adult children, a son, Thomas, and a daughter, Sandy, who is in her thirties and has young-onset PD. Although Jim would have preferred to leave assets equally to his two children on his death, given the uncertainty about the progression of Sandy's PD and the economic impact on her career, Jim is not sure that this is fair. Some of the new research endeavors to treat PD leave Jim cautiously optimistic that Sandy's PD might not progress to a level that will require him to distribute his estate primarily to Sandy. Obviously, though, the future is unknown, and Jim is naturally cautious about how much reliance to place on those research possibilities. After reviewing the matter with the family, Jim opts for the following disposition scheme in his will: 50% to Sandy, 45% to Thomas, and 5% to MJFF. When Jim discusses this plan with his attorney, a couple of important issues are raised. While the likelihood exists that Sandy will need more financial assistance, that really cannot be known for certain because the progression of her disease is unknown, and new therapies are being developed. Just as important, Jim's attorney points out that there is no certainty that Thomas will not face some type of financial, health, or other adversity during his lifetime. Finally, Jim's attorney explains that if a percentage of his estate is left to charity, the will and estate financial reporting must be submitted to the state's attorney general's office to comply with state law. This can create costs, complications, and disclosures that Jim is not thrilled about. Further, the attorney points out, valuation issues can arise if a percentage of an estate is left to charity. Jim anticipates that the family vacation home in the country will be kept by both Thomas and Sandy for them and their children to use. For estate tax purposes, the children have the incentive to value the house as low as possible to minimize tax costs. However, the charity selected, as an independent charity, is obligated to ensure that fair market values are used. This disparity in goals could create some friction. The combination of these and other issues, the attorney explains, makes a donation of a percentage of the estate potentially problematic. Therefore, Jim settles on the following disposition scheme:

- A fixed dollar bequest of $500,000 in his will to the charity he selects, to be used to fund research efforts in which Sandy has been interested
- The remaining estate is divided as follows:
    - 40% to each of Thomas and Sandy, in a separate trust designed to meet the specific needs of each child.

- The remaining 20% of the estate distributed to a "pot" trust, which can benefit any child or grandchild based on need.

This will enable Jim to distribute his estate in equal portions but also ensure that if Sandy, or even Thomas, has more demanding issues, funds can be distributed to address those issues. The children and the designated charity all benefit from this revised plan.

Insurance Trust

A common estate planning tool is to establish a trust that purchases insurance on your life. The advantage of this approach is that the proceeds of the insurance will not be taxed in your estate on death, and the proceeds can be protected from claimants of your heirs. For families with a child with PD, an insurance trust can be used as a means of providing extra protection for that child.

> ✸ EXAMPLE: Janice Gordon has three children, two daughters and a son, Phillip, who has young-onset PD. Janice is adamant that her will bequeath assets equally because she does not want to create any animosity or jealously among her children. Janice is especially concerned about keeping the peace because her daughters have been wonderfully supportive and helpful to her son, and she wants to encourage that. However, Janice realistically

understands that Phillip might not be able to work for more than a limited career span. Thus, although his training as a CPA would have provided him with a good living, the PD is likely to undermine that. While it is uncertain what trajectory Phillip's PD will take, Janice wants to ensure for him what she believes to be an adequate lifestyle. While Janice's will bequeaths all assets to her children equally, she takes special steps to protect Phillip. Janice establishes an *irrevocable* (cannot be changed) *life insurance trust* (ILIT) that purchases a $2 million universal policy on her life. This trust is designed to help support and supplement Phillip. If Phillip and his wife have children, the funds remaining in the trust will be distributed to his children following his death. Janice feels that this is important because Phillip may not have the capacity to earn a livelihood to support his children and cannot obtain life insurance because of his PD. If Phillip dies without children, various charities are named as the beneficiaries of the remaining insurance proceeds.

Charitable Lead Trust

A *charitable lead trust* (CLT) is designed to benefit charity and, at the same time, provide a future gift (inheritance) to your child at a substantially reduced gift (estate) tax cost. When you set up a CLT, the named charity receives the income (actually an annuity payment) for a number of years that you agree to (the longer the number of years, the greater the gift tax break); thereafter, the assets in the trust will be distributed to your child. This is a great mechanism to benefit charity, protect your child, and achieve tremendous tax savings. CLTs are a planned giving mechanism that is particularly consistent with the objectives of the MJFF—to accelerate better treatments and ultimately a cure for PD. This is so because a CLT typically pays an annual annuity to a charity for a specified number of years, and the remainder inures to the benefit of your child. CLTs are also an ideal technique when asset values and interest rates are low. More details on this technique are explained in later chapters.

> ❂ EXAMPLE: Shifra Stein, a widow, has a substantial estate. Her son and only heir, David, is age 52 and has PD. He continues to work and is self supporting, although his income is declining because his symptoms have made it more difficult to work the hours he has been accustomed to. Shifra wants both to reduce the potentially substantial estate tax she faces and also ensure her son's financial future. Shifra establishes a *charitable lead annuity trust* (CLAT) for her son. Shifra has her attorney prepare a trust agreement and obtain a tax identification number. The trustee sets up an account with the wealth management firm Shifra has used for many years. Shifra then donates $1 million dollars to the CLAT. The named charity will receive $60,000 per year for the next 25 years. Shifra directs that this be used to address specific charitable objectives that she feels strongly about as long as the charity deems a need for such goals. She does not receive an income tax

charitable contribution deduction at the time of the gift (although if she had structured the CLAT as a grantor trust, she could). Assume that Shifra has made prior gifts to her heirs totaling $800,000, using up $800,000 of the $1 million gift tax exclusion available (the amount any taxpayer can gift without a gift tax). A $1 million gift could generate nearly $400,000 in gift tax cost [($1 million gift − $200,000 remaining exclusion) × 50% assumed tax rate]. However, because of the annuity payment of $60,000 per year for 25 years, the value of the eventual gift to her son David is reduced. Had Shifra set up such a CLAT in 2007, the gift would have been reduced to about $200,000, and no gift tax would be due on the transfer. Because of the decline in interest rates, if Shifra had set up such a CLAT in May 2009, she could shorten the duration of the charitable lead interest (the number of years the charity would receive $60,000 prior to her son David receiving the balance of the trust) to 20 years, and the value of the gift to David would have been only $56,000. The lower interest rates would have enhanced the gift tax advantages of the CLAT. From a personal perspective, not only has Shifra provided substantial benefit to her chosen charity, but she also has provided a retirement plan for her son to ensure his financial security into old age. In 20 or 25 years (depending on when the CLAT was funded), when David reaches age 60 or 65, the CLAT will end, and he will receive a distribution of the remaining trust assets. Shifra's wealth manager believes that it is reasonable for her to realize a 7.5% return on the CLAT portfolio, given the long time horizon. As such, her son David will receive not the original $1 million she gave to the CLAT, but possibly in excess of $2 million when the trust terminates. Shifra is confident that this amount will more than adequately fund her son's retirement years.

Charitable Remainder Trust

A *charitable remainder trust* (CRT) is almost exclusively thought of as a tax planning technique to benefit you as the donor and your spouse, if you are married. However, the CRT technique can be used to benefit a child as well, although there will be a gift tax consequence to this use. You'll have to be sure that your estate planner structures the trust to provide at least 10% of the initial value of the property you donate to the CRT to charity so that the trust will meet tax law requirements. If you merely name your children (or perhaps just a child living with PD) as a beneficiary, a gift tax may be due on formation of the trust. This gift tax consequence can be avoided if you retain in your will the right to terminate the children's interests under the CRT. This step, however, will cause the value of the CRT assets to be included in your estate at death. If you don't have a spouse, or if your spouse's life expectancy is limited, perhaps because of complications of his or her PD, this technique could be particularly useful. Depending on how the calculations play out, your heirs actually could receive a better economic arrangement using this approach than had you simply sold an appreciated asset, paid capital gains tax, and retained the proceeds to be included in your taxable estate.

You can take several steps to protect a child with PD and in many cases can weave in provisions to benefit your favored charities. The preceding examples illustrate only a few of the myriad of planning possibilities.

Grandchild

The financial planning for a grandchild with young-onset PD is similar to planning for a child with PD, with some exceptions. The most significant tax exception, and one that can have a tremendous impact on planning, is that gifts to grandchildren face severe restrictions if they are to avoid the *generation-skipping transfer* (GST) *tax*. This tax can be almost confiscatory in nature and must be addressed carefully by your estate planning attorney and accountant in any planning you undertake. The GST tax applies to transfers you make to *skip persons*. In layperson's terms, this includes grandchildren, trusts that only have grandchildren as beneficiaries, and other persons that are brought within the definition of skip persons. The objective of the GST tax is to prevent very wealthy taxpayers from circumventing the estate tax by bequeathing assets down the generational line. For example, if you bequeathed half your estate to your grandchildren, those assets could not be taxed first in your child's estate, thus avoiding the estate tax at your child's level. The GST tax in simplistic terms seeks to tax transfers to grandchildren (or other skip persons) as if they had been included in the child's estate. You are permitted to exclude from GST tax an amount called the *GST exclusion,* which is presently $3.5 million (the same as the amount of estate exclusion).

Let's look at the same planning ideas discussed for your child with PD earlier and see how they differ if you are endeavoring to assist a grandchild.

Power of Attorney

As explained earlier, your power of attorney designates a person (agent) to manage your financial, legal, and other affairs if you cannot do so. Your agent cannot spend money or make gifts for a grandchild unless you specifically authorize it. This contrasts with payments for a minor child, which your agent might be able to make without an express authorization. This may be the case because your state's laws may make it your legal obligation to support your minor children, so your agent would have the authority to make the necessary payments. Thus, for a grandchild with PD, it's even more important that you're clear as to what your agent can spend your funds on. You could authorize gifts to grandchildren, but any gifts in excess of the annual gift tax exclusion ($13,000 in 2009, but the amount is inflation indexed) will have a gift and possibly a GST tax consequence as well. Direct payments for tuition and medical expenses can be made without any gift tax or GST tax consequences if you authorize your agent to make them. For a grandchild, the direct payment of medical expenses by your agent could be a tremendous help to the grandchild and a significant gift tax break for your estate.

You should also address the issue of equality of gifts and other distributions in the document. Do you care if one grandchild receives more than another?

Will

Your will should probably include a trust to protect your grandchild/beneficiary who is living with young-onset PD. The trust can provide for the management of assets in the event your grandchild reaches a point at which he or she cannot easily manage his or her own financial affairs, similar to the decisions discussed earlier concerning a child. You should address with the attorney drafting your will whether the trust should be a *special needs trust* (SNT) depending on your grandchild's financial and health condition. This decision could be much more difficult to make for a grandchild, given his or her younger age and perhaps greater uncertainty as to the future. A significant difference in planning for a grandchild, as opposed to a child, is the potential for GST tax. If total bequests to grandchildren exceed the GST exemption available to you ($3.5 million in 2009, but future increases or decreases are uncertain), your estate could face a substantial GST tax. Thus your will is likely to be more complex in that your estate planner will draft it so that the maximum bequests to grandchildren and trusts for grandchildren won't exceed the maximum GST exemption to which you are entitled. In many cases, the ability to make distributions for tuition and medical expenses can add some flexibility to provide for a grandchild with PD without unduly complicating your estate plan. Bear in mind that gifts during your lifetime will be limited further by the $1 million gift exclusion.

✪ EXAMPLE: Juan and Maria Hernandez have two adult children and four grandchildren, one of whom, Jesus, was diagnosed recently with young-onset PD. At this stage, they are not certain what Jesus' needs will be. The Hernandezes also want to fund a gift to a charity that funds research targeted to those with young-onset PD. After reviewing various planning options with their attorney, the Hernandezes opt for a fairly standard estate plan. On the death of the first of Juan or Maria, the maximum assets will be distributed to a *bypass trust,* with the balance to a marital trust (QTIP trust designed to qualify for the unlimited estate tax marital deduction). The bypass trust is designed to benefit the surviving spouse but ensure that those assets are not included in the estate of the surviving spouse. Under current law, $3.5 million can be contributed to such a trust. Be cautious, because this amount may increase or decrease in future years, and many states provide much lower thresholds before they assess a tax. To provide flexibility, the trustee of the bypass trust is authorized to make distributions to any of Juan and Maria's children, but to avoid GST issues, grandchildren are excluded from this general distribution provision. In addition, the Hernandezes added the right for a trustee to distribute any monies directly to those providing medical or education benefits to Jesus because such distributions won't trigger GST issues. The right to make distributions to Jesus' parents, as well as direct medical and education distributions, will provide flexibility and a safety net for Jesus. Rather than complicate their estate plan with charitable deductions, and especially in light of their desire to fund programs and research directed at young-onset PD now, the Hernandezes simply make a cash gift to the charities they wish to benefit.

Insurance Trust

The use of a life insurance trust to benefit a child with PD was discussed earlier. When the goal is to benefit a grandchild, the GST tax also should be considered. In many such situations, it will not be possible to qualify gifts to the insurance trust for the annual GST gift exemption, so your accountant may have to file a gift tax return each year to allocate the GST exemption. Don't worry about these technicalities—your accountant will be equipped to address them for you. The next example will illustrate the planning, not the technicalities.

⚙ E X A M P L E : Jeff and Susan Smith have three children and two grandchildren, including a granddaughter Christy, who has young-onset PD. Jeff and Susan have their estate planner prepare an insurance trust primarily to benefit Christy. They have the trust purchase a $1 million survivorship (also called *second-to-die*) policy. This policy pays only when the last of Jeff and Susan dies. It is substantially less costly than buying a policy on only one of their lives. Importantly, while either Jeff or Susan is alive, they are confident that they can provide any extra help Christy needs. They are really only worried about providing for Christy after their deaths, so survivorship insurance fits the bill. Because Christy's parents are successful in their own right, Jeff and Susan view this policy as simply an extra safety net for Christy and a way of showing Christy their love and emotional support. As a result, they have authorized the trustees of Christy's trust to make distributions to charities that Christy recommends. On Christy's death, all remaining insurance proceeds in the trust are to be distributed to named charities. Jeff and Susan understand that there is no tax advantage to these donations because the funds are outside their estate, and the insurance trust is unlikely to get much income tax benefit, but their goal is to help Christy and certain charitable causes, not only to achieve tax benefits.

Charitable Lead Trust

A *charitable lead annuity trust* (CLAT) was discussed and illustrated earlier within the context of providing benefit to a child with PD and a benefit to charity. For a grandchild, this technique won't be practical because of the GST tax discussed earlier. While many of the technical nuances are beyond the scope of this book, and an estate planner and accountant can deal with them, the valuable planning ideas that can help you to achieve your personal and charitable goals can still be illustrated. For a gift to a grandchild of the assets remaining in a CLT after the charity's lead interest, you'll probably use a *charitable lead unitrust* (CLUT). A CLUT is a trust designed to benefit charity and, at the same time, provide a future gift (inheritance) to your grandchild at a reduced gift (or estate) and GST tax cost. When you set up a CLUT, the named charity receives the income (actually a unitrust payment) for a number of years that you agree to (the longer the number of years, the greater is the tax break). Thereafter, the assets in the trust are distributed to your grandchild. This is a great mechanism to benefit a charity, protect your grandchild, and achieve tax savings. A unitrust payment is a fixed percentage of the value of the trust determined each year.

✪ E X A M P L E : You set up a CLUT paying 6.5%. The trust pays the named charity 6.5% of the value of the assets each year. If the trust has $1 million in assets, the charity receives a payment of $65,000. If, next year, the assets grow to $1.2 million, the charity receives a payment of 6.5% × $1.2 million, or $78,000. This potential for the increasing distributions to charity each year with a CLUT reduces the amount that will be received at the end of the CLT term by the grandchild as opposed to what a CLAT would be provide. This is the basis of why the tax laws permit the allocation of the GST exemption when a CLUT is funded but not for when a CLAT is funded.

✪ E X A M P L E : Maria D'Angelo has a substantial estate, is concerned about estate tax, but wants to provide a safety net for her grandson, Anthony. She has her estate planner create a 25-year CLUT, to which she gifts $1 million. She does not receive a charitable contribution deduction, but for gift tax purposes, her eventual gift to Anthony is reduced from $1 million to under $190,000. This reduction results from the payments that will be made to charity for 20 years. Her accountant will file a gift tax return using up about $190,000 of her gift and GST tax exemptions. The charity will receive an annuity payment each year based on 6.5% of the fair value of the assets in the trust in that year. The first year's payment (assuming a full year) will be $65,000. After the twenty-fifth year, the entire value of the trust will be distributed to Anthony (or, if Maria prefers, a trust for Anthony's benefit). If the trust assets grow at 7.5% year, Anthony should receive about $1,170,000. Thus Maria has provided a significant benefit to charity and used that benefit to leverage a gift and GST tax beneficial safety net and retirement plan for her grandson.

Using Charitable Donations to Leverage GST Transfers to Benefit Your Grandchildren

Your estate is quite large, and you want to benefit your grandchildren and perhaps later descendants, but the GST tax makes that quite difficult and costly. Unrelated to that objective, you support various charitable causes. You might be able help your grandchildren and benefit charity simultaneously. To accomplish this, you must combine charitable planning with planning for your grandchildren to avoid the harsh impact of the GST tax. This technique can enable you to provide for the future educational and medical expenses of your grandchildren without triggering the GST tax that you would have to endure if you did not combine the charitable gift with this planning. Since you intended to make charitable donations in any event, there is no real incremental cost to using this planning to leverage gifts to benefit your grandchildren.

Assume that you want to pass wealth on to your grandchildren and, in particular, provide for the medical care of your grandchild, perhaps one living with PD. The simple solution would be to set up a trust to pay for your grandchildren's tuition and medical costs and give substantial assets to that trust. However, because the only beneficiaries of such a trust are your grandchildren, every dollar you give to the trust would be subject to the GST tax. In tax parlance, the trust itself would be classified as a *skip person,* so all gifts to it would be subject to the GST tax. To avoid this tax cost, you would have to allocate (use up) your GST exemption. Your GST exemption is a tax benefit that lets you transfer up to a certain amount of assets to grandchildren (or trusts for them) without incurring the GST tax. A common theme of planning, especially for larger estates, is to preserve as much of your exemption amount for later gifts or at least to save it for situations where it really must be used. If you've already used up your GST exemption, the tax cost of transferring assets to a trust only for your grandchildren would be prohibitive.

So how can you set up a trust to provide for tuition and medical costs of your grandchildren and not trigger the confiscatory GST tax? Because it is assumed that you want to make charitable donations, you can use this fact to avoid the GST tax on transferring assets to a trust for your grandchildren. How? Structure the trust to benefit charity as well as your grandchildren. If, for example, you provide that on your death 25% of the trust will be given to specified charities, the trust is now designed to benefit a combination of your grandchildren and charities, so the trust will not be classified as a skip person for GST tax purposes. The result is that your gifts to the trust will not trigger the GST tax. Your trustee can be given the discretion to pay medical and tuition expenses for your descendants forever. This can include, for example, all the medical costs of a grandchild with PD. As discussed earlier (see "Power of Attorney"), direct payments of tuition or medical expenses for your grandchildren are not subject to gift or GST tax. In tax terminology, these payments are not treated as taxable distributions from a trust that would trigger GST tax. Thus no GST tax is applicable on the gifts you make to the trust by virtue of the inclusion of charitable beneficiaries (although you'll have to plan with your tax adviser to address gift tax issues). There is no GST tax on payments of tuition or medical expenses because of the exceptions provided in the tax laws for these payments. On your death, the named charities will receive 25% of the trust assets. The trust will continue to benefit your grandchildren (and even later descendants) by paying trust monies for tuition and medical costs. Tax problem is solved. Grandchildren and charity benefited. Discuss the risks and issues of this type of plan with your advisors.

You can take numerous other steps to protect a grandchild with PD and, in many cases, weave in provisions to benefit charity. The preceding examples illustrate only a few of the many options. The tremendous complexity that the GST tax creates, however, really requires expert advice from your tax advisers.

Partner/Friend

If you have a friend or partner that you wish to benefit or protect, or if you have PD and you have a nonmarried partner, you'll need to address certain legal and tax issues. Planning is quite different when a nonspouse significant other or partner is involved. Most state laws won't provide you with the same protection. The federal tax and other laws, such as the Defense of Marriage Act (DOMA), provide no flexibility or protection for a nonmarried partner. Some aspects of the planning might be helped by combining your planning with charitable giving, but in all events you'll need expert tax and local state law–specific advice. The following discussion reviews possibilities based on some of the estate planning documents you might use in your own planning.

Power of Attorney

This common estate planning document designates a person (agent) to manage your financial, legal, and other affairs if you cannot do so. If you have a nonmarried partner, it's even more important that you get in place a comprehensive, signed, durable power of attorney because a partner in most instances will not enjoy the same presumptions or powers under state law that a spouse would. Thus the power of attorney could be more important to ensure that your partner can assist you when you have difficulties. If your partner has PD, you could incorporate specific provisions into your power of attorney permitting your agent to support your partner. Any support or gifts in excess of the annual gift tax exclusion ($13,000 in 2009, but the amount is inflation indexed) will be subject to tax. A nonmarried partner does not qualify for the unlimited gifts that a spouse would. Your agent can make direct payments for medical or educational expenses without limit and without gift tax consequences. While you are tailoring your power of attorney to address assisting your partner, give some consideration to having your lawyer modify the gift provisions to include the right to make charitable gifts.

Revocable Living Trust

Many people use *revocable living trusts* to avoid probate, although a far more important use is to manage assets during illness or disability. If your family did not support your relationship, using a revocable living trust might enable you and your partner to avoid some of the family entanglements if one of you becomes incapacitated or dies. If you have a revocable living trust as part of your estate plan, be sure to have your attorney make modifications similar to those described for a power of attorney, including the right to make charitable gifts and purchase charitable gift annuities, if you wish.

Will

Your will probably should include a trust to protect your partner who has PD. The trust can provide for the management of assets in advance of when your partner reaches a point at which he or she cannot easily manage his or her own financial affairs. This is particularly important in the event that your illness or death prevents you from helping at that time. A trust also might ensure some insulation and protection in the event that you or your partner's family seeks to undermine the bequest. Because bequests to a partner do not qualify for the unlimited estate tax marital deduction, additional legal steps and, depending on the size of your estate, more aggressive tax minimization techniques might be necessary. As with all estate planning documents, your will can provide a wonderful opportunity to tailor a charitable bequest. With a nonmarried partner, a charitable bequest can be a great way to minimize estate tax costs.

> ✪ EXAMPLE: Jane Smith, in her mid-70s, has an estate of $5 million. Her partner, Maureen McGrath, age 61, has PD. Jane and Maureen live in a state that only permits a $1 million estate tax exclusion, so $4 million of assets will be subject to state estate tax, even if only $1.5 million is subject to federal tax ($5 million – $3.5 million exclusion). Jane would like to provide protection for Maureen in the event of her death, minimize estate taxes, and benefit several charities. Maureen is insistent on trying to avoid estate tax not only to minimize taxes but also because of what she views as the unfairness that a nonmarried partner could face almost a 50% estate tax burden, whereas a married partner would have no estate tax. Jane knows that the first $3.5 million of her estate will pass to Maureen free of

estate tax in 2009 (but that figure may change in the future). Jane wants to minimize the estate tax on the remaining $1.5 million of her estate while benefiting both Maureen and charity. To accomplish these goals, Jane provides that on her death, $1 million of her estate will be paid to a *charitable lead annuity trust* (CLAT) to benefit charity for 15 years and thereafter to benefit her partner Maureen. If $1 million is given to a 15-year CLAT paying 6.0%, or $60,000, annually to charity (with payments at the beginning of the year), the value of the eventual gift to Maureen will be reduced to about $270,000 (assuming that today's interests rates apply). This substantial reduction for estate tax purposes is because of the 15 years of payments to charity. The remainder of her estate, after payments for executor commissions (to Maureen), will be paid to Maureen in a lifetime trust. Jane believes that the lifetime trust approach will provide Maureen with protection if she needs it, but while Maureen is able, she is named as a cotrustee with another friend. The combination of the estate tax exclusion ($3.5 million in 2009, but may increase or decrease) and the CLAT deduction will almost eliminate the federal estate tax. The use of trusts likely will minimize outside interference and protect Maureen. The payments of $60,000 per year will provide for charitable causes that are important to both Jane and Maureen.

Insurance Trust

The use of insurance trusts is especially common among nonmarried partners because it provides a safe, nontaxable means of addressing the estate tax (because no marital deduction is available). For nonmarried partners, especially when one of you has PD, an insurance trust can be used as a means to provide extra protection and address any estate tax issues.

> ✪ E X A M P L E : Michael Jones and Gordon Green are partners. Michael owns a shore home worth several million dollars, as well as other assets. While both Michael and Gordon work full time, Gordon's PD symptoms have progressed, and it is not clear how long he will continue to work. Both Michael and Gordon are concerned about the estate tax that will be due if Michael dies first and leaves the shore home to Gordon. Michael has his estate planner set up an *irrevocable life insurance trust* (ILIT), and the trust purchases $2.5 million of insurance on Michael's life. If Michael dies before Gordon, the insurance will fund the payment of the estate tax and ensure enough capital to generate a cash flow to support Gordon when he has to stop working. On Gordon's later death, any remaining monies will be given to charity. If Gordon dies before Michael, Michael will stop paying on the insurance policy, and the trustee will either cash the policy in or sell it in the secondary market and distribute the proceeds to charity.

You can take a host of other steps to protect a nonmarried partner with PD and often in a manner that supports charitable causes that are important to you. The preceding examples only illustrate a few of the opportunities.

Chapter Summary

Who do you want to help? Who are you worried about? What is your connection to PD? This chapter has identified a number of possible relationships you might have with someone affected by PD, whether yourself, your spouse, or a child, grandchild, partner, or other person. You can take affirmative steps to help and protect that person, often in a manner that can benefit charities that are important to you. In some situations, your charitable donation actually can enhance the benefits you are able to provide to the person you are seeking to benefit. It truly can be a win-win situation.

> **CAUTION:** Most planning ideas presented in this chapter are complex and must be implemented with the advice of your accountant, estate planning attorney, insurance consultant, investment adviser, wealth manager, and other experts. Be sure to review all the requirements and potential issues and drawbacks to any of the techniques suggested before proceeding.

CHAPTER FOUR

DIFFERENT ASSETS
CAN BE USED TO HELP
FUND THE CURE

M OST DONORS ASSUME that their choice of how to make a donation is limited to using a check or credit card. While either works, almost any asset can be used to make a donation. If you consider the wide range of assets that can be donated and some of the personal, legal, and tax benefits that donating different assets (not just a check) can provide, you might be willing to structure a more sophisticated and larger donation while simultaneously accomplishing several planning objectives.

Sometimes the easiest perspective for you or another prospective donor to take is to focus on a particular asset. You may have a certain asset that you want to give to charity or gift part and sell part. You may have read something about a planning technique involving that asset, and you want to explore your options. In many cases, your interest is piqued by a conversation on the golf green about something miraculous your golfing partner achieved by donating a particular asset. This chapter will help you to identify some of the planning opportunities available for many of the different assets you are likely to own. We'll start with the most common asset donation—cash—and then explore more complicated assets.

Cash, Check, Credit Card Payment

The Most Common Donations Are Not Always the Simplest

A cash donation is the simplest and most common type of gift for charity. A tax deduction generally is received for the cash contributed. From a practical perspective, cash donations are easy to make. They also are generally simple from a tax perspective—write a check, get a deduction. But alas, in the Alice in Wonderland world of tax rules, few things don't have exceptions, special rules, and other twists and turns pertaining to them. Although this book does not focus on tax technicalities, and the few covered are relegated to Chapter 6, an exception will be made here to illustrate that what you might assume to be a simple cash gift is not always so simple. The take-home message is that if some of the other techniques described in this book sound complex, in many cases, they are not much more complicated than the "simple" cash donation. This is not to dissuade you from making a donation by check or credit card but rather to encourage you to explore more sophisticated planned giving and gifts of assets that require more planning.

So you write a check or give a credit card number to charity. What issues might affect your deduction?

Donations Reduced by Benefits Received

If a benefit is received in return for the donation, the value of your deduction must be reduced.

    ✪ EXAMPLE: You pay $500 to attend an event organized by a Team Fox member. As an attendee, you receive a gift bag. If the fair value of the gift bag is $100, you are entitled to a $400 tax deduction.

If you attend a gala black-tie dinner as a sponsor, for example, the $5,000 you paid for a pair of tickets must be reduced by the cost of the dinner, say, $500, leaving a donation of $4,500. The charity should notify you of the amount of your payment that is a qualified donation. Many charitable events provide attendees with gift bags and souvenirs. The tax law provides an exception for gifts of modest value, so these may not reduce the amount of your charitable contribution deduction.

Cash Bequest in Your Will

A cash bequest to charity in your will is assumed to provide for an estate tax charitable contribution deduction. However, this ignores the reality that very few estates are actually subject to federal estate tax. Federal estate tax, in fact, affects at most only a few percent of those who pass away in a given year. Therefore, if you were to make a donation under your will, unless your estate exceeds $3.5 million (the estate tax applicable exclusion in 2009, which might be changed by future tax legislation), you may not realize any federal estate tax benefit from a charitable donation. A simple solution might be for you to leave the money intended for charity outright to your heirs, and ask them to make the donation. This request would not be legally binding on them, merely morally binding. They may qualify for an income tax deduction, which is a better tax break than a zero estate tax benefit. With the likelihood of future income tax increases on wealthier taxpayers, this income tax deduction might be worth even more in future years than it would be now. If your estate is taxable, a different result may occur.

⊗ EXAMPLE: For decades, Fran Worthington has been a donor to The MJFF. However, for the past few years, she has not been a significant donor because she wants to preserve assets for her own needs. She remains worried about the course of her Parkinson's disease (PD) and what types of medical and other care expenses she may incur that are not covered by insurance. In her will, Fran would like to leave a $100,000 bequest to MJFF. When Fran reviews her will with her attorney, her estate is valued at $1.4 million. She lives in a state with no estate tax. The $100,000 will not provide any income or estate tax benefit, but it will increase the legal fees on the administration of her estate. If a bequest is made under Fran's will, the formalities of notifying the charity, obtaining a receipt from the charity, and so on easily could add costs to the administration of her estate. Because Fran's heirs are her three nephews, whom she trusts fully, she opts not to leave the bequest in her will. Instead, she has her attorney add a clause to her power of attorney authorizing her agents to make a donation to MJFF in the amount of $100,000. She writes a side letter to her nephews asking them to make sure that MJFF receives the $100,000 donation and that if the full donation wasn't made by her while she was alive and well, or by her agent under her power during her disability, they should complete the intended donation to MJFF in equal one-third amounts sufficient to bring the total payments up to $100,000. In her letter, she advises them not to count any small donations under $500 as having been paid toward the $100,000 pledge.

When Is Your Donation Deductible?

If you write a check to charity, it's deductible in the year you mail it or unconditionally give it to the organization as long as it clears the bank in due course. If you make a payment by credit card, your donation is deductible in the year you incur the charge, even if you pay the actual credit card bill in a later year. Thus, if you're looking to get a deduction in late December, you might be better off using a credit card or, if you send a check, using certified mail to prove the mailing date.

Numerous other restrictions and limitations affect cash and all other donations. An overview of some of these technicalities is presented in Chapter 6.

Deferred or Planned Cash Donations

Cash donations also can be planned and paid over time so that you can make a more significant current commitment without undue financial pressure.

✪ EXAMPLE: Yolanda Frank is tremendously appreciative of all the help that a particular charity has provided for her since her recent PD diagnosis. She wants to send a big thank-you to the volunteers and professionals at the charity, but her financial resources are somewhat limited. She signs a pledge agreement for a $10,000 pledge payable at the rate of $1,000 per year because of her concerns about the economy but which she hopes to pay at the rate of $2,500 per year over four years if those concerns prove unfounded. This enables her to send that big thank-you and make a contribution that really makes her feel good.

Life Insurance

Great Way to Make a Larger Contribution

You would really like to make a long-term and meaningful commitment to charity, but you don't have the financial strength to write a big check today. Don't give up the thought of a larger donation: You may be able use life insurance to accomplish your goal in an affordable manner. It's a great "feel good" way to help charity. It's an effective way to demonstrate long-term commitment to a charity that, during economically difficult times, could use the arrangement to encourage other donors. Insurance can provide a great example of giving back for your children and others who look to you for guidance.

Buy a New Policy for Charity

You can buy a permanent insurance policy that will be owned by a charity of your choosing and for which that charity is named beneficiary. Each year, you make a contribution to that charity that is sufficient for it to pay the premium. You get an income tax charitable contribution deduction for the gift. The charity owns the policy, pays the premium with your donation, and is the beneficiary. In the meantime, the cash value of the policy grows as an asset of the charity. You will have made a large gift that you can pay over time. But don't reduce your annual gifts to the charity because of this. The insurance policy should be an *additional gift* because the charity won't be getting current dollars that it can use from the cash you donate for the premium payments.

❂ EXAMPLE: John Smith's sister Julie has PD. John doesn't have the financial wherewithal to make a large gift to a particular charity that has advocated for people with PD but wants to show his sister support. John, age 30, applies for a $100,000 life insurance policy, naming the charity as owner and beneficiary. The premiums for a policy that will be fully paid in 10 years are only $1,000 per year. Each year, John donates $1,000 to the charity, which pays the premium. After a 40% income tax deduction, John's out-of-pocket cost for a $100,000 bequest in honor of his sister Julie is only about $600 per year.

Donate an Existing Policy

Instead of having a new policy purchased by you in the name of a charity, you could donate to the organization an existing policy that you no longer need.

⚙ EXAMPLE: Jason Cutter's youngest child just graduated college. Jason has several insurance policies, including an old $500,000 universal life, which he had purchased to ensure adequate resources for his children's college costs. Since his family's need for the policy has been obviated, Jason donates the policy to the charity. While Jason might be able to sell the policy to investors, he's uncomfortable with unknown investors owning an insurance policy on his life and therefore prefers the charitable route. Be careful if this is a significant concern of yours in that many charities may opt not to hold a policy but rather to sell it to raise current funds for use in meeting their charitable objectives.

⚙ EXAMPLE: Several years ago, Charles Wong had purchased an insurance policy to cover anticipated estate tax costs and particularly to ensure that his closely held business could be passed on intact to his heirs. Since the federal estate tax exclusion was increased from $1 million several years ago to $3.5 million in 2009, Charles realizes that he no longer needs the policy. Instead of cashing in the policy, he opts for the charitable route and donates the policy to a charity. Because the policy has been generously funded, it is anticipated that the charity will not have to make future payments to keep it in force.

Restrictions and Issues That Affect Insurance Donations

A few considerations could affect your insurance planning, some of which are noted here. These issues highlight a common cautionary thread throughout this book: You need professional guidance to implement any planning ideas. You cannot have any rights (incidence of ownership) in the insurance policy you donate. If you do, your contributions to pay for the policy will not qualify as tax deductions. Before completing the donation of any insurance policy, have your estate planner confirm that the charity can legally own (have an insurable interest in) an insurance policy on your life under state law. When donating an insurance policy, your income tax charitable contribution deduction probably will be based on the premiums you previously paid into the policy. You may not qualify for a contribution deduction for the full fair market value of the policy. Be wary of more complex charitable insurance plans because many of them are fraught with problems. Some problematic plans include charitable *insurance split-dollar schemes* and arrangements, whereby a charity partners with an investor group to buy insurance on your life to profit both the investors and the charity. There are several variations of charitable/insurance schemes, and you probably should reject them all unless your estate planner vets and approves them. Clear any charitable insurance plan with your estate planning attorney before proceeding to assure both you and the charity that the plan will succeed without creating headaches you're not looking for. Finally, expect that the charity will undertake considerable due diligence on any policy before it can accept it as a donation.

Marketable Securities

Donating Appreciated Securities

You can always sell stocks and donate the proceeds to charity. It's simple, but it does not always provide the best tax result. Publicly traded stock is valued at the average of the highest and lowest selling prices on the date you make the contribution. When you donate stock, your contribution deduction is based on the fair value of the stock donated.

> ❂ EXAMPLE: Freda Swarez has owned stock in a well-known bank for years. The stock was purchased at $20 per share and is now worth $140 per share. Freda could sell the stock and donate the proceeds to charity, but she would pay a capital gains tax on the gain of $120 per share. If, as many tax advisers believe, capital gains rates will increase in future years, this cost will increase as well. Instead, Freda directs her broker to transfer the stock to a charity. This is a simple no-cost process. Freda has no capital gains to report because she sold no stock. Freda, however, can claim a charitable contribution deduction on her personal income tax return of $140 per share.

Don't Donate Depreciated Securities

The tax benefits and simplicity of donating appreciated stock make it an ideal way to benefit charity and yourself. However, don't assume that all stock donations are beneficial. If you own stock that has declined in value and donate it, you won't benefit from any of the loss for tax purposes. For losers, you're better off selling the security, recognizing your capital loss for income tax purposes (for whatever benefit you can get), and donating as much of the cash proceeds as you wish to charity. Unfortunately, as a result of recent economic conditions, many prospective donors have security losses, so the best approach might be to plan your harvesting of gains and losses and donations in coordination with your accountant and investment manager.

For Really Big Gains, Consider a Charitable Remainder Trust

If you have very substantial gains on a large stock position, more sophisticated planning may be called for.

> ✪ EXAMPLE: Ira Frankovich purchased 100,000 shares of a startup research company, BreakThru Research, Inc. (BRT), for $1 per share. The company has developed a new drug that has just received Food and Drug Administration approval, and the stock price has shot up to $57 per share on an unadjusted basis. Ira's gain is huge, $5.6 million. The stock pays almost no

dividends. Ira is retiring and needs more income to cover living expenses. He also wishes to diversify his investment holdings because they have become such a substantial portion of his estate. However, to sell his BRT stock would trigger substantial capital gains. Ira works out a more comprehensive plan.

- Ira will contribute 40,000 shares, worth $2,240,000, to an exchange fund sponsored by a major investment firm. This will enable him to receive income tax–free limited partnership interests, diversify his portfolio, and have an asset that is ideally suited for other family estate tax planning transactions.
- Ira will sell 20,000 shares at $1,120,000 and pay capital gains tax. This will provide him with a cash pool to use as he wishes.
- Ira will retain 20,000 shares because he still likes BRT's prospects.
- Ira, age 67, will donate 20,000 shares to a *charitable remainder trust* (CRT), which he will structure to provide a 5% payout. The CRT shares will be sold income tax–free by the trust, and the proceeds will be reinvested by the trust in a diversified portfolio. Ira will receive back an annual payment of $50,000 for the rest of his life. Ira will realize a charitable contribution deduction of about $400,000, which will help to offset part of the gain on the sale of his BRT shares. Most important, Ira will be sharing some of his windfall with charity and helping the charity to fund research projects of particular interest to him.

- Because of his charitable goals, Ira structured the CRT with only a 5% payout to himself. He anticipates that his wealth manager will earn at least 6.5% on the CRT investments. Thus, at the end of Ira's life expectancy, the charity should receive in excess of $1.3 million. The financial and charitable benefits are significant.

Clothing and Household Items

Contributions of clothing and household items must be in good used condition or better. Items of modest value may, by regulation, be denied any deduction. Most charities, including MJFF, will not accept such donations. Paintings, antiques, art, jewelry, and items valued at over $500, for which a qualified appraisal is obtained, are excluded from these new restrictions. Because of the administrative costs associated with these types of property donations, smaller-value property will have to be donated to charities that can effectively handle such donations. A detailed list and photographs of any such items should be retained.

Personal Property

The ability to donate *personal property,* such as art, jewelry, furniture, cars, and so forth, opens up new opportunities for donations to help charities. Here, we'll review some of the planning opportunities and rules for these types of donations. Because of the administrative efforts and costs associated with personal property donations, many charities, including MJFF, will first have to evaluate the feasibility of accommodating such donations. Acceptance may depend on the cost and time of accepting such a gift relative to the value of the property involved. The key point is that if you have property that you wish to donate, explore the options with the charity of your choice. If you're flexible, a method that maximizes your tax and personal objectives and benefits important charitable causes can be found.

Donating Tangible Property

Gifts of *tangible personal property* are simple to describe, and they may be simple to conclude, but personal-property gifts are subject to myriad restrictions and reporting requirements. Personal property includes such items as antique furniture, artwork, jewelry, and so forth (not land or buildings). Detailed rules are provided for the appraisal of property contributions, reporting requirements (which vary based on the nature and value of the property donated), restrictions on deductions for personal property (limited to a percentage of your income, etc.), and more (see Chapter 6). Although you can deduct the current value (fair market value) of many of the assets you contribute to charity, this is not always the case with tangible personal property. These rules should not deter you from donating tangible property: Rather, they simply should encourage you to keep your accountant involved in monitoring the process and its consequences.

Donating Tangible Property Unrelated to the Charity's Tax-Exempt Purpose

Property Whose Use Is Not Related to the Charity's Tax-Exempt Function: If you contribute appreciated tangible property, such as a painting, to a charity other than one that could display the painting as part of its charitable function (e.g., an art museum), your income tax deduction will be limited to what you paid for the property (your *adjusted tax basis*), not the fair market value of the property, if the property's use by the charity is not related to its tax-exempt purpose or function.

Property Whose Use Is Related to the Charity's Tax-Exempt Function: If you contribute appreciated tangible property, and the property's use by charity is related to its tax-exempt purpose or function, such as antique furniture used in a PD center waiting room, your income tax deduction will be the fair market value of the property (not just what you paid for it). However, if the charity disposes of the property within three years of your contribution, your income tax charitable contribution benefit will be adjusted downward from fair value back to your cost (*adjusted tax basis*) unless the charity certifies that the property was to be used for furthering its purpose or function but that use became impossible to implement. In most, but not all, situations, it is unlikely that MJFF would be an appropriate charity for such a gift.

Fractional Interests in Personal Property

Although you can donate a *fractional interest* in tangible personal property, such as a painting, the restrictions on these donations are so severe that it is not likely to be a practical approach. If you donate a fractional interest in personal property to charity, the organization must receive full ownership prior to the date of your death (get out the Ouija board) or 10 years. If you make a later contribution of the balance of the property to charity, your deduction for income, gift, and estate tax purposes is the lesser of value at the time of your initial contribution or the value at the date of your subsequent contribution. If the value of the property increases, your deduction remains limited to the earlier value. Talk to your accountant before proceeding with this type of gift.

Retirement Plan Assets

Bequests of IRA and Retirement Plan Assets

Individual retirement account (IRA) and other retirement plan assets are great assets to use to fund a bequest to charity. On your death, if your estate is large enough, retirement plan assets are subject to a double tax: income tax on distribution to your heirs and estate tax. Although with careful planning the income tax costs can be stretched out, the tax deferred, and to some extent, estate taxes mitigated by using IRA and retirement plan assets to fund estate tax–oriented trusts, the benefit of donating these assets remains substantial. This is a great way to benefit charity with an asset that might net only a very small percentage of dollars to your heir after all taxes are considered. Also, it avoids any issues of your needing the money during your lifetime, so it's a great charitable giving technique if you are living with the challenges of PD. If your spouse lives with PD, the same technique can be used, but the charity could be named as the remainder beneficiary after your spouse dies.

The method in which to make such a donation is to name the charity as a beneficiary of the IRA or other retirement plan that you wish to donate. This planning can be facilitated by the following:

- Consider splitting your IRA account so that you have a charity as the sole beneficiary of one account. For example, if you have a $1 million IRA and want to leave $500,000 to your only daughter and $500,000 to charity, split the IRA, and name the charity as beneficiary of one account and your daughter as the beneficiary of the other. If this is not done prior to death, the IRA might be able to be divided or the charity interest paid out prior to September 30 of the year following your death to avoid undermining your daughter being able to stretch out payments from her portion of the IRA.
- Sign a beneficiary designation listing your intended charity as beneficiary.
- Have your advisers determine whether your spouse must provide a written consent to your leaving your retirement plan to charity instead of to him or her.

- Sign a pledge form with the charity so that it is alerted to your intent and commitment.
- Revise your power of attorney to clearly exclude from your agent the power to change the beneficiary designation for the IRA or retirement plan involved to remove the charity (or if you specifically want this flexibility, include a clause saying so).
- Review the planning with your financial planner and accountant. You might opt to purchase life insurance to supplement the inheritance to your heirs or take other steps. Also, they can review the many technical nuances of this type of planning with you.
- Be certain that the use of IRA or retirement plan assets is carefully planned. For example, if your executor (personal representative) satisfies a specific dollar charitable bequest under your will (*pecuniary bequest*) with an IRA, taxable income could be triggered inadvertently and your hoped-for tax benefits defeated. This is so because if your executor satisfied a pecuniary bequest with retirement assets subject to income tax (*income in respect of a decedent*, or IRD), gain must be recognized. Instead, make the intended charity a specific beneficiary of your IRA, or have a provision in your will or trust mandating the use of your IRA to pay your bequest to charity with the IRA.

Lifetime Donation of IRA and Retirement Plan Assets

The flexibility of permitting donors to contribute IRA funds to charities while the donors are alive is a long-sought benefit by many charities. Congress finally provided some relief, but the window for this benefit was only enacted for 2006–2007 and then extended through 2009, although there is hope that the benefit will be extended to future years or made permanent. This benefit has a host of technical requirements, including the need for the plan sponsor's cooperation.

- This leniency provision applies only to IRAs, not to other types of plans.
- Individuals age 70.5 or older may gift up to $100,000 in each of 2006 through 2009 to charity. You must have passed your half-birthday before consummating the donation. It is not sufficient that the donation be made in the year that you turn 70.5.
- The donation must be made directly from the plan trustee to charity to qualify.
- The donation must have otherwise qualified to be deductible-in-full as a charitable contribution deduction.
- You must obtain a written confirmation of the donation and that no goods or services were received in exchange for it.

Except for this new rule, the distribution from the IRA would have to be included in your gross income to qualify. If you meet all the requirements, the IRA donation is not included in your income. The result is that any limitations on contributions won't limit the tax benefit of such a contribution. This issue had been a significant deterrent to charitable gifts of IRA assets in that the entire IRA distribution may have been taxable but only a portion deductible, thus generating an income tax cost for trying to make a contribution. The limitations on charitable contributions based on your adjusted gross income (AGI) discussed in Chapter 6 are a prime factor in this. Another problem was the phaseout of itemized deductions based on gross income. The inclusion in gross income of IRA funds withdrawn thus could result in a decrease in other deductions.

- The donations will count toward any required minimum distributions, although the need to make *required minimum distributions* (RMDs) in 2009 was suspended.
- The amount of IRA qualified charitable distribution does not also provide a contribution deduction. The charity cannot be a donor-advised fund, supporting organization, or split-interest entity. Thus only public charities, of which MJFF is one, qualify for this benefit.

Although the benefits of this provision are tremendous, the restrictions and limitations make its use very limited. Hopefully, Congress will see fit to expand this benefit, make the requirements more reasonable, and make it a permanent fixture of the tax laws.

Family and Closely Held Businesses

Family and closely held (a few owners) equity (stock in a corporation, membership interests in a limited-liability company, etc.) can present many unique and valuable charitable giving opportunities.

Business Inventory

Inventory can be a great donation to support any particular charity and the PD community generally. Donating needed equipment or supplies for research programs can provide a great boost to those efforts. Donating items used at a fund-raising auction, products to be used as gifts to donors at a major event (e.g,. bags, gift items, or product samples), can be a tremendous help in building the excitement and success of a charitable fund-raising event. These types of donations might be useful to a Team Fox fund-raising event, but generally, MJFF is not equipped to accept inventory donations.

What type of deduction can you obtain for donating inventory? The general rule is that if the property, if sold, would generate ordinary income (not capital gains), your charitable contribution deduction is limited. The limitation is the lesser of the fair value of the property you donate or what you paid for the property (adjusted tax basis). Because the amount of your deduction is limited to what you paid for the property, the complex rules (discussed earlier) about whether the charity used the property for its exempt purpose are not relevant. If your corporation donates inventory to a particular charity in the year it is manufactured, your corporation claims its deduction as part of the cost of goods sold, not as a charitable contribution deduction. This is a valuable benefit in that corporate contributions are limited to 10% of income, but deductions as cost of goods sold are not limited at all. If you're a sole proprietor, this deduction as a cost of goods sold can save you self-employment taxes.

A special rule permits a larger deduction if the inventory is donated for the care of the ill, needs of minors, or use in the charity's exempt purpose. Qualifying donations permit you to deduct your cost (tax basis) plus half the appreciation (but not more than twice your cost).

Charitable Bailout of Closely Held Stock

Donations directly to a named charity or to a charitable remainder trust to benefit a particular charity can have special use when a key asset is stock in a closely held business. A *charitable bailout* of a closely held business' stock can address important planning problems for a closely held business owner. Stock in a closely held corporation can be difficult or impossible to sell because outsiders generally will be very reluctant to own a minority interest in a close business. Another problem could relate to the type of corporation involved. Assume that the corporation is a C corporation (i.e., not an S corporation) and has available cash that you would like to donate to charity. However, it may not be practical to make a dividend distribution to provide the cash for such a donation because a dividend distribution will result in double taxation (the corporation first pays tax on the earnings, and then you pay tax again on receipt of the net earnings in the form of a dividend). Another common problem scenario for a closely held business is when a parent owns stock in a close corporation and wishes to transfer control to a child without triggering income tax on redemption. One possible solution for this latter scenario is called a *stock bailout*. You can make a gift of any portion of the stock in your corporation to a charity. At some later date, the charity may, in its sole discretion, sell some of this stock back to your corporation. This provides you with a charitable contribution deduction for income tax purposes for the stock donated. The charity eventually can receive a cash amount for the contribution. When the corporation redeems the stock, the interests of the children owning the stock will increase because the charitable bailout/redemption of your stock will increase their relative ownership interest.

✪ EXAMPLE: Paul Clintwood owns stock in a family manufacturing business. Over the years, he has made gifts of stock, using the annual gift tax exclusion, to his three children who are actively involved in the business. Paul now owns about 60% of the stock, and he would like to reduce his ownership to below 50%. Paul has the corporation appraised, as well as the value of a 12% interest in the corporation. Paul could sell the stock to his children, but that would trigger capital gains tax and would add assets back to his estate, which is inconsistent with his estate planning objectives. Paul confers with the intended charity. After appropriate due diligence, representations, and warranties from Paul and an opinion from tax and legal counsel, the charity agrees to accept the stock donation. Paul then makes a donation of 12% of the outstanding stock to the charity. At some later date, the charity may choose to sell some of this stock back to the corporation. These steps could provide Paul with a charitable contribution deduction for the stock donated. When Paul's corporation repurchases stock from the charity, that stock becomes *treasury stock,* and it is no longer relevant to the determination of ownership percentages in the company. This reduces Paul's ownership to 54.5% (60% – 12%/100% – 12%), closer to his goal. A few more annual gifts of stock might suffice to complete the reduction of his ownership interests to less than 50%. The charity eventually should be able to receive cash when it sells the stock back to the corporation.

A number of issues must be addressed with this type of planning. The charity cannot be obligated to sell any portion of the stock back to the corporation. All sales must be made at its discretion. If a prearranged plan for the resale of the stock exists, it can be difficult to differentiate whether the charity was obligated inappropriately. If the charity is not under any legal obligation to resell the stock it receives, there is a possibility that it could sell the stock to another person (even one of your competitors), vote the shares in a manner inconsistent with your desires, and so on. This technique cannot be used for S corporations. Properly planned, a charitable bailout can be a helpful technique.

Business Advertising Expense

A commonly overlooked opportunity might simplify and enhance your deductions for supporting a particular charitable cause. In some instances, you might be able to characterize cash payments or property donations to charity as business advertising expenses. This might prove valuable because it avoids the numerous and complex rules and limitations that affect charitable contribution deductions. If the payments your business makes to a charity bear a direct relationship to your business, and these payments were made with the reasonable expectation of a financial return commensurate with the payments, then the amounts can be deducted as business advertising (an ordinary and necessary trade or business expense). For example, if your business were to sponsor a golf tee at a Team Fox golf event, the cost of your listing of the business sponsorship might be characterized as a business advertising expense.

Principal Residence or Farm

Generally, you can only obtain a charitable contribution deduction if you donate your entire interest in a particular property to charity. There are, however, several exceptions, including an important one relating to your home. You can make a donation today of an interest in your personal residence or farm that only takes effect in the future. This special rule permits you to claim a current income tax deduction without the legal costs and complications of setting up a trust to do so. Thus you can contribute your house to charity and continue to live in it for the remainder of your life or for some set number of years that you choose. Your spouse could also reside in the house as well. The gift of the house to charity, however, must be permanent (irrevocable). You can use these rules to donate your house, cooperative apartment, or even vacation home to your chosen charity. A donation of a remainder interest in a farm, which includes land and buildings, also qualifies. Charities will require a due-diligence and evaluation process to accept such donations. Donations of fixtures, furniture, and other personal assets in the house or on the farm will not qualify.

> ✪ EXAMPLE: Donna Freytag has PD. She resides in a ranch house that is completely accessible. She hopes to continue to live in her home for the rest of her life. Because she is single, her hope is to help charities serving those with PD. As her business has improved, her savings have grown, but her PD symptoms also have progressed. Donna realizes that this is an opportune personal time to sell her business. She feels that it is becoming too hard to work the hours necessary and that the value of the business has grown to the point that it should fund her early retirement. Donna donates her home to charity, retaining a *life estate,* which gives her the right to live in her home for the remainder of her life. The income tax deduction she realizes on the donation of the remainder interest in her home offsets some of the tax cost she will incur on selling her business. Thus Donna is able to bank more of the proceeds from the sale of her business for her retirement while ensuring a wonderful future gift for several charities that are important to her.

The value of your income tax deduction for donating a remainder interest in your home or farm is rather complex to calculate, and you'll want the assistance of your accountant.

The deduction will consider that portion of the donation classified as land value and that portion classified as building value.

Commercial Real Estate

Commercial or investment real estate is a common asset used in more complex charitable plans. A number of special issues and provisions affect real estate donations. The following discussion summarizes a few of them. An important threshold issue is that in light of all the problems that can arise with property subject to hazardous waste or other litigation issues, no charity will accept a donation of real estate until it has had ample time to perform due diligence and make sure that no title, environmental, or other problems exist. The administrative and other costs of accepting such a donation will have to be factored into the charity's analysis of whether the donation is viable to accept.

State transfer and deed taxes may not apply to transfers of real estate to a charitable organization. This can provide a substantial savings when compared with an actual sale. If you own real properties in several states directly (rather than through a limited-liability company, partnership, or other entity), your estate will face ancillary probate in those other states and, depending on that state's tax system, additional estate or inheritance tax. If a property instead is donated to charity, even in the form of a charitable remainder trust so that you will receive a continued income (cash flow in the form of an annuity or *unitrust* payment) stream, the ancillary probate and tax problem is avoided.

If the property being donated was depreciated (writing off a portion of the purchase price each year over the time period permitted by the tax laws), then depreciation recapture (recharacterization of some portion of the gain attributable to depreciation) can cause additional problems by reducing the amount of your charitable contribution deduction. This technicality should be reviewed with your accountant.

If you donate real estate to your private foundation rather than to a public charity, such as the MJFF (which is a public charity), you might not qualify for a deduction equal to the full value of the property donated. Donations to public charities are not subject to this limitation. Your income tax deduction is limited in the case of certain capital gain property.

Real estate contributions in which the property has appreciated are subject to a limitation that your deduction cannot exceed 30% of your *adjusted gross income* (AGI). An exception exists if you donate real estate to a public charity: A special election can be made to reduce the contribution by the amount of gain that would have been classified as *long-term capital gain* (see Chapter 6). If the property is donated to a private charity, a 20% limitation applies.

A donation of real estate subject to a mortgage is treated as being partially a gift and partially a sale. The amount of mortgage on the property that the donor is relieved of is treated as an amount realized (as if it were additional sale proceeds). This rule applies even when nonrecourse financing is used.

❂ EXAMPLE: Steven Callaghan owns a small retail strip shopping center worth $1 million, which he developed at a cost of $765,000. His adjusted tax basis in the property (cost to build less depreciation) is only $100,000. Steven donates the property to charity, subject to a nonrecourse first mortgage of $500,000. Steven is treated as if he sold the property and realized $500,000, the amount of the mortgage, less an allocable share of his $100,000 basis. The basis is allocated using the relative values of the mortgage and the fair market value of the property. Because the mortgage of $500,000 is one-half the value of the $1 million value, 50% of the developer's *adjusted tax basis* of $100,000 ($50,000) is allocated against the amount realized. Thus Steven has a gain of $450,000 [$500,000 – ($500,000/$1,000,000 × $100,000)] on the donation.

Generally, a donor cannot obtain a deduction for a charitable contribution of less than an entire interest in property.

❂ EXAMPLE: Dana Smith permits a charity to use his vacant land for overflow parking for a major fund-raising event. The value of this use can readily be estimated from prices of nearby parking facilities. No deduction is permitted because this is a donation of a nonqualifying partial interest in property.

This exception does not apply where the partial interest is the entire interest of the donor. An undivided part interest in property can qualify for a charitable contribution deduction. For example, a donation of 10 acres of a 35-acre parcel or 40% of an income interest in a property in which you don't have any other interests will qualify without limit. Special rules apply to remainder interests in a personal residence or farm (see earlier discussion).

Leveraged (mortgaged) real estate presents significant tax issues to any type of estate, charitable, or related planning. The donation of mortgaged real estate to charity may trigger taxable gain because the amount of the mortgage is treated as sales proceeds, as if a portion of the property were sold, not donated.

> ✪ E X A M P L E : Lissette Norman purchased investment land many years ago for $200,000, taking out a $150,000 mortgage to complete the purchase. The mortgage has been paid down to $100,000. The property is now worth $1 million, and Lissette wants to donate it to charity to use for the construction of a new research facility that will be conducting research financed by private-equity partners. Lissette is deemed to have received proceeds on making the donation of $100,000, the amount of the mortgage. These proceeds are offset by a pro rata portion of Lissette's $200,000 tax basis of $20,000 ($100,000 mortgage/$1,000,000 fair value × $200,000 basis).

Chapter Summary

Whatever real estate, business, or other assets you own and are willing to use to benefit charitable causes, a charitable plan can be created to achieve optimal tax savings for you and your loved ones, meet other important personal goals, and benefit your intended charities and their important causes. Each asset creates its own charitable giving issues and opportunities. This chapter has surveyed many common assets and hopefully given you ideas on how you can use different assets to benefit charity. As with all planning, advice of your tax adviser, accountant, estate planner, and possibly business or real estate lawyer may be necessary to implement the plan properly. For many of the assets discussed in this chapter, your advisers may have to coordinate details with the recipient charity and even determine if the charity can feasibly accept the property.

CHAPTER FIVE

MEET PERSONAL GOALS WHILE FUNDING THE CURE

W HAT GOALS AND OBJECTIVES motivate your charitable giving and other financial and estate planning? Benefiting charity can be a presumed goal of any compassionate or caring person. However, if your other goals and objectives can be met while simultaneously benefiting charity, your willingness and ability to contribute should be even greater. If you can identify the specific goals you have, the concerns that worry you, and the objectives you want to meet, a plan often can be crafted to accomplish several of your objectives. With some creativity, even goals that appear on the surface to be inconsistent sometimes can be melded into a single plan that substantially meets all of them. Chapter 3 evaluated ways to coordinate charitable giving to benefit specific people who are important to you. Chapter 4 evaluated ways to use specific assets to accomplish personal and charitable goals. This chapter evaluates the common goals many donors have, perhaps providing you with some ideas and guidance about how you can meet similar goals. While there is redundancy among the three chapters, the goal is to help you to quickly and easily identify charitable planning strategies from whatever perspective is the most comfortable for you.

Ensuring You'll Have Enough Cash Flow (Income)

For many prospective donors, the key impediment to making a larger gift—and a key planning goal when structuring a large donation—is to ensure the donor adequate cash flow for personal needs. If this is a concern for you, dedicating some portion of your investments and directing some portion of your charitable giving using *charitable remainder trusts* (CRTs), and/or *charitable gift annuities* (CGAs) may make sense.

Using a Charitable Remainder Trust to Create Cash Flow

A CRT can be a tremendous estate and financial planning vehicle to generate cash flow. There are three ways a CRT can help your cash flow:

1. A CRT is a charitable trust to which you contribute assets, typically appreciated assets. You obtain a current income charitable contribution deduction based on the expected value of the eventual donation to charity, which generates cash flow.
2. The CRT can sell the appreciated assets you donate without triggering any tax. That preserves cash flow.
3. Finally, the CRT can pay you a periodic payment for a specified number of years or for your life. This provides cash flow that could be used to meet your living expenses. This can be as a periodic annuity (CRAT) or as a percentage of the value of assets each year in the CRT, called a *unitrust payment* (CRUT).

If you anticipate a kick-up in inflation in future years, the CRUT is better for your long-term cash flow because you will participate in the increase in the value of assets held in the trust. An example illustrates this plan.

✪ EXAMPLE: Sean Fitzgerald, whose brother has PD, purchased XYZ, Inc., stock in 2001 for $10 per share. The value per share is now $1,000. The stock pays almost no dividends. Sean is retiring and needs more income to cover living expenses. He also wishes to diversify his XYZ, Inc. holdings because they have become such a substantial portion of his estate. However, to sell XYZ, Inc. stock would trigger a substantial capital gains tax. Sean also is interested in helping to fund additional PD research efforts that could revolutionize PD treatment. Instead of selling the stock, Sean could donate it to a CRT and receive back a monthly payment for life (and even for the life of his wife as well). The charities pursuing this research that he named could sell the stock and invest in a diversified portfolio designed to generate cash flow to meet the periodic payments to Sean. The CRT will not have to recognize any capital gains tax of $990 per share on the sale. As a result, Sean can effectively have the entire investment, undiminished by capital gains tax, working to generate his monthly income. If Sean and his wife are age 72 and 68, respectively, a CRT could pay them yearly installments of about $50,000 for life. They also would receive a charitable deduction of a bit under $200,000. The financial benefits are potentially significant. While Sean could also consider other techniques, such as an exchange fund, those approaches won't accomplish his charitable goals.

Gift Annuities Generate Cash Flow

Charitable gift annuities (CGAs) are a popular form of charitable giving and, in many respects, are simplified versions of the CRT just discussed. You could make a donation of appreciated stock (and avoid the capital gains tax) or a gift of cash to a charity in exchange for payment of a fixed amount (an annuity) for your life. You can even structure the gift annuity to pay a fixed amount to you and your spouse for your joint lives. In favorable contrast to a CRT, you can arrange for a charitable gift annuity directly with any charity that issues them without the complexity or legal costs associated with a CRT. However, the simplicity and lower cost have a price—loss of flexibility and a higher payout presumed to the charity (which may be a positive depending on your perspective).

If you donate appreciated property to a charity in exchange for a charitable gift annuity, you will recognize only a portion of the taxable gain that you would have realized had the property been sold as you receive annuity payments. You'll also obtain a charitable contribution deduction that is calculated based on a formula that factors in your age, life expectancy, and other factors (actuarial calculations).

Creating a Retirement Plan Using Charitable Giving

Charitable giving can be used in several ways to create the equivalent of a retirement plan. A special type of *charitable unitrust remainder trust* (CRUT) called a *net income makeup unitrust*

(NIM-CRUT) can be used to benefit a charity *and* create the equivalent of a retirement plan for yourself. A *charitable lead annuity trust* (CLAT) can be used to create something analogous to a retirement plan for your child.

Charitable Remainder Unitrust as a Retirement Plan

A CRT was described in previous chapters. In simple terms, a typical CRT arrangement has you contribute appreciated stock to the CRT. The CRT sells the stock and does not pay capital gains tax because a CRT is tax-exempt. The CRT then invests the proceeds and pays you an annuity for life. A couple of spins on this "plain vanilla" CRT can turn a CRT into a means of providing a retirement plan–like benefit to you, all while still benefiting your favorite charities. First, some background.

A CRT can be structured as an *annuity trust* (CRAT) that pays you a fixed amount each year of your life. If you gave $1 million to a CRAT structured to pay a 6% annuity, you would receive $60,000 every year. A CRT can also be structured as a unitrust (a *charitable remainder unitrust,* or CRUT) that pays an amount each year based on a fixed percentage of each year's value of the CRUT's assets. Therefore, if the 6% CRUT paid the same $60,000 in its first year, and the value of the stocks it held increased to $1.5 million by next year, the CRUT would pay you 6% of this figure, or $90,000. A couple of additional twists to go.

A CRUT can also be structured as an income-only unitrust. This modified form of CRUT can be used to provide you a *net-income-only arrangement*. Using this type of CRUT, you, as the income beneficiary, receive only the actual trust income if the income is less than the fixed percentage payment required (e.g., 6% of the principal of the trust). This is a *net-income CRUT* (NI-CRUT).

The NI-CRUT type of trust also can include a *makeup provision*. This is called a *net-income makeup CRUT* (NIM-CRUT). In early years, actual income might be less than the 6% required CRUT payment. In later years, if the net income of the CRUT exceeds the specified percentage of trust assets required to be paid (e.g., 6%), this excess can then be paid to you—as the income beneficiary—to make up for the shortfall in prior years. The shortfall is determined based on the difference between the amounts actually paid in prior years and the amounts that were required to have been paid based on the fixed percentage. The key is to intentionally fund a NIM-CRUT with assets that won't generate much income initially, coupled with this makeup of the shortfall after your retirement. This concept can best be illustrated with an example.

⊗ EXAMPLE: Daniel Williams has a substantial income, is getting on in years, and wishes to provide for his favorite charity. Daniel expects to retire in five years. On retirement, Daniel expects his income to drop significantly, placing him in a lower income tax bracket. Daniel establishes a net-income-only charitable remainder unitrust arrangement with a makeup provision (a NIM-CRUT). Daniel funds the trust with a $1 million initial contribution. Daniel receives a current income tax deduction while he is in his prime earning years and highest marginal tax bracket. The trustee of the CRUT invests the $1 million in low-dividend-paying growth stocks (or perhaps Daniel contributed private equity or real estate holdings that generate no cash flow but which should be readily salable by the five-year retirement mark). The unitrust percentage is set at the lowest permissible amount that complies with tax law requirements (5%). The dividends on the stock portfolio produce a mere 0.75% return, or $7,500, which is paid to Daniel each year. After year 5, Daniel retires. The stock portfolio, which has appreciated to $1.5 million, is liquidated and invested in high-yield bond instruments, real estate investment trusts (REITs), and other income-oriented investments. These income investments produce a cash return of 8%, or $120,000. Daniel is entitled to distributions of 5% of the $1.5 million CRUT asset value based on the unitrust amount selected when the trust agreement was signed, or $75,000. However, as a result of the makeup provision, Daniel can be paid additional amounts in each of the remaining years of the trust to make up for the shortfall in prior, preretirement years. Daniel's shortfall would have totaled $212,500. This is the excess of what Daniel should have been paid had the CRUT produced enough income: [5 years × (5% × $1 million value)] = $250,000, over what Daniel actually received in each of those years (5 years × $7,500 = $37,500). Daniel will be entitled to all the income from the income-only unitrust for a number of years to come, until this shortfall is repaid. Once it is repaid, Daniel will still be entitled to 5% of the value of the CRUT in each year. By having deferred $212,500 of income to his retirement years, Daniel may save income taxes because of his lower postretirement income tax bracket. He also has shifted significant income to a time period when he will need it. If Daniel anticipates that his income tax rate may rise in future years, this tax bracket arbitrage could prove negligible or even negative.

A Charitable Lead Trust Can Create a Retirement Plan for Your Child

A CLT is a technique generally used to minimize the gift tax costs on large transfers to your children. In some instances, a CLT can be structured to be taxed to you (a *grantor trust*) so that you can realize a contribution deduction for the donations it makes. However, a CLT also can be used in a manner intended to generate something akin to a retirement plan for your child.

   ⊗   E X A M P L E : Moesha Smith, M.D., has a daughter with young-onset PD, age 37, who is presently working. Moesha is concerned that because of the PD, her daughter will be able to work only a limited number of additional years. Moesha is also keenly aware of recent advances in medical research that show promise of helping her daughter. Moesha establishes a CLT to pay a fixed 6% amount, $60,000, annually to MJFF for the next 20 years.

The payments over this term period eliminate almost any gift tax impact on Moesha's transferring $1 million to the CLT (the present value of the gift is reduced to about $56,000). In 20 years, when her daughter is age 57, the CLT ends, and an early retirement plan will be available to help her. Moesha anticipates that the $1 million should increase substantially before her daughter's anticipated retirement at age 57. Meanwhile, Moesha is optimistic that the $60,000 per year to the MJFF will help to fund valuable research efforts directed at identifying neuroprotective therapies.

Create a Safety Net for Family Medical Expenses

You can set up a trust to provide a safety net to cover medical costs of your entire family while avoiding the costly *generation-skipping transfer* (GST) *tax* and still benefiting charities of your choice. This concept was discussed in Chapter 3 and is illustrated here with an example.

✪ EXAMPLE: Mahmood Johnson has his estate planner structure a trust to benefit his grandchildren and later descendants, as well as several charities. On Mahmood's death, 25% of the trust assets (the *corpus*) will be divided among the several charities listed. Prior to Mahmood's death, all the trust will be available to pay for medical expenses for his descendants. After Mahmood's death, the three-quarters of the trust assets remaining after the donation to charities will continue to be used forever to pay for medical costs for his grandchildren and later descendants. This trust will be formed in a state that has eliminated any laws limiting the duration for which a trust can last (*rule against perpetuities*). The trustee Mahmood names will be given the discretion to pay medical expenses for his grandchildren and future descendants. This can include, for example, all the medical costs of a grandchild with PD. These direct payments of medical expenses for Mahmood's grandchildren are not subject to gift or GST tax.

Employment for an Heir

If you're very charitably inclined, have the financial wherewithal to make substantial gifts, and have specific charitable goals you would like to meet, a private foundation may be an ideal planning technique for you. With the exercise of caution and reason, in some instances it is feasible to have your private foundation employ family members in the management and operation of the foundation and make grants to appropriate charities, including the funding of specific PD research projects directly or in conjunction with existing

PD organizations, such as MJFF. This can provide your children or other heirs with the following benefits:

- Training in philanthropy to help them better understand their obligations to society in general and charity in particular and how to deal with the wealth you anticipate eventually leaving to them.
- The foundation board may include outside experts active in fields of PD research and programming to help guide your heirs in the optimal support of projects to benefit organizations providing support services for people with PD, research, or other issues.
- The responsibility, pride, and confidence of being actively engaged in responsible charitable endeavors.
- Compensation commensurate with the services they provide, their skills and abilities, and so on.
- The ability to control family wealth that you contribute to the foundation and for which you receive an income tax deduction for many years in the future. Because a foundation is only required to distribute 5% of its assets for charitable purposes each year, the large donations you contribute could continue to grow even while annual donations are distributed, as long as your foundation realizes more than 5% return on its investments.

A private foundation is a private charity. Because it is not public, the tax laws impose a host of specific requirements that must be met. Failure to meet these requirements can cause substantial tax costs and penalties. If the compensation paid to your heirs is not reasonable, it could be viewed as an act of self-dealing, and a tax of 10% could be imposed. If the excessive or inappropriate compensation is not refunded, the tax could be 200% of the amount paid. You also should be aware that the tax form filed by your foundation, Form 990-PF, is a public document that can be viewed by anyone. If, subject to these and other limitations and caveats, you are comfortable with the approach, a private foundation can provide reasonable compensation and employment for your heirs.

Donating Without Diminishing an Heir's Inheritance

Insurance Can Be Used to Replace Assets Donated

You might be willing to make a substantial contribution to charity but are concerned about the impact the contribution will have on your heirs. In many instances, you might be satisfied to address this concern by combining a life insurance plan with your charitable donation. This is often done whether the donation to your selected charities is outright, in a *charitable remainder trust* (CRT), or made using other techniques. Insurance planning is frequently combined with charitable planning to replace the value of the property donated to the charity with insurance passing to your heirs. In fact, this approach is so common that the trust often used to hold life insurance intended to replace the assets you donate to charity is commonly called a *wealth-replacement trust*. It replaces the wealth you've given to the organization through other techniques. In reality, it is no different in structure and use than most *irrevocable life insurance trusts* (ILITs); it is just used in this specific manner.

Insurance Planning and Your Charitable Remainder Trust

This concept is often used when you make a donation to charity using a CRT because the CRT provides you with the cash flow to buy insurance to replace the assets donated. The CRT technique was illustrated in several earlier examples; here, the focus is on coordinating the CRT with insurance so that your heirs still receive a significant inheritance, even though you made a large charitable gift. You fund a CRT with appreciated assets and receive an income (annuity or unitrust) stream back. You then use some portion of this increased cash-flow stream to fund (make gifts to) an *irrevocable life insurance trust* (ILIT) for the benefit of your heirs (e.g., your children).

This plan enables you to meet your desired charitable goals of providing for a favored cause while preserving or even enhancing the wealth you can ultimately transfer to your heirs. Wealth transfer can be increased because the insurance held by your ILIT generally will not be taxable in your estate. The income tax savings you should realize from the charitable contribution deduction should provide you with cash flow. You can use some or all of that tax savings cash flow to make gifts to an ILIT to enable it to purchase insurance on your life. The trustee of the ILIT can purchase insurance on your life (or, if you are married, second-to-die life insurance on the lives of both you and your spouse) in an amount sufficient to replace the value of the assets that you donated to charity or to a CRT designed to benefit the organization.

⊛ EXAMPLE: Sheila Rinaldi donates real estate to a CRT that eventually will benefit a specific charity. She will avoid a substantial capital gains tax when the CRT sells the property. The proceeds will be invested, and Sheila will receive an annual income (really cash flow because it is an annuity or unitrust payment, not income). Sheila will use some of this cash flow from the CRT to make annual gifts to an ILIT. The trustee of the trust will use the proceeds to buy life insurance on Sheila's life sufficient to replace some portion or all of the value of the donated property to Sheila's son and daughter after her death. This is sufficient to replace the $1 million worth of real estate Sheila transferred to the CRT. The children will receive the same $1 million on Sheila's death that they would have received had the planning not been undertaken. However, had no planning been undertaken, the real estate that the children would have received may have been reduced by a 50% marginal estate tax. Thus the children actually may receive more than double the net value with the charitable/insurance plan than without it. This is a winner.

⊛ EXAMPLE: In 2007, Fernando Alvarez, age 65, owned non-income-producing property worth $1 million, which he purchased for $200,000. He gave the property to a CRT, which generated a $417,000 contribution deduction. This provided an income tax savings of approximately $140,000. Further, Fernando will avoid approximately $220,000 in immediate capital gains tax on the sale of the property. With no further planning, the property would have been included in Fernando's estate, generating a $500,000 state and federal estate tax. The CRT will pay Fernando $60,000 per year for his life. Fernando can make annual gifts to his son, daughter-in-law, and two grandchildren (or to a different trust designed to own insurance) totaling $40,000, using most of the annual gift tax exclusion (he can gift up to $13,000 in 2009 to any number of people each year with no gift tax consequence). This amount can be used by the children to purchase $1 million in life insurance on Fernando's life, sufficient to replace the $1 million property given to the CRT. Fernando's heirs will receive the same $1 million on his death that they would have received had the planning not been undertaken. While there are a number of simplifying assumptions being made here, the plan can provide considerable benefits from many perspectives.

Using Life Insurance to Protect a Charitable Remainder Trust's Cash Flow

The preceding discussion showed how you can use life insurance to replace the value of assets you donate directly to a charity or to a CRT to benefit a qualified charity. Another financial risk exists. A key financial benefit of a CRT is the periodic cash flow (annuity or unitrust) you receive for life or for a specific period of years. Implicit in this planning is the idea that you will survive long enough to receive sufficient distributions to make the plan viable. If you die prematurely, you'll have received few distributions. Further, if you have children or others who depend on you financially and who are not beneficiaries of the CRT, your death will terminate the cash-flow distribution they were indirectly depending on. This risk is one you might be able to address with an insurance plan. In the appropriate circumstances, the charitable remainder technique can be combined with a life insurance policy insuring the life of the income beneficiary (or *life beneficiary*) of the CRT. If you die prematurely, the insurance proceeds can replace the CRT cash-flow stream that your family will have lost as a result of your death (remember, the CRT payments might be structured to pay you for life, and then the principal reverts to charity). This could be done, for example, with a life insurance trust for the benefit of your spouse and/or children. The life insurance trust should be structured to ensure that the proceeds are not included in your taxable estate. In some cases, an insurance arrangement providing for decreasing coverage (to approximate the decline in the loss of expected income as you live through the intended term of the trust) can be used.

Using Charitable Giving to Teach Your Heirs the Value of Charitable Giving

Estate planning not only should be about the transmission of wealth, but it also should be about the transmission of values, particularly philanthropy, to your heirs. There are many ways for you to accomplish this lofty goal—a goal that can provide considerable benefit to your heirs. Consider the following:

- Establish trusts under your will that direct your heirs to distribute some specified amount or percentage of the trust each year to charities. You could provide guidance about how this should be done and select at least one of the trustees who has the skills and personality to help inculcate charitable values and guide your heirs in these endeavors.
- Set up a private foundation and actively involve your heirs in serving on the board of directors to allocate charitable gifts.
- Set up and then make a donation to a *donor-advised fund* (DAF) and designate your heirs in the DAF agreement as the people responsible for making the decisions about which charitable causes should be benefited.
- Establish a *charitable lead trust* (CLT) and have the funds that are required to be distributed each year allocated at the direction of your heirs.

You can set up guidelines, even quite specific ones, within any of these documents designating how, when, and for what purposes charitable gifts should be dispersed. For example:

- If you want to specifically benefit MJFF, you could articulate this. Bear in mind, though, that the somewhat unique objective of MJFF of funding specific PD research goals could be impeded if you empower your heir to direct in too great detail how MJFF can use the funds.

- If, instead, you prefer to benefit any charities providing research to cure PD or programs for people living with PD, you could specify that parameter.
- If you preferred to fund specific types of programs, you could provide that parameter to guide your donations.

Chapter Summary

This chapter has provided a review of many common donor goals that can be met as part of an overall charitable, financial, and estate plan. Charitable planning is not only about maximizing your tax deductions. It also can be about myriad personal and financial goals ranging from inculcating charitable giving values in your heirs, to maximizing your cash flow, to creating a retirement plan, and more. Flexible and creative planning can help you to achieve a range of goals and encourage and facilitate even greater donations.

CHAPTER SIX

TAX RULES
FOR
CHARITABLE GIVING

A NUMBER OF TECHNICAL TAX RULES affect your donations to charity and the amount of tax benefit you may qualify for. Bear in mind that there are a number of tax bills pending, and new tax legislation is anticipated. Most tax pundits anticipate higher rates and more restrictions on deductions and techniques for the wealthy. Therefore, be sure to review the actual impact on your tax position of any proposed charitable gift with your tax advisers before proceeding. Although we have intentionally tried to minimize discussions of these many technical rules—focusing instead on planning ideas to help you achieve your charitable and personal goals—this chapter is the exception. Here, we'll overview many significant tax rules. Although it is assumed that you'll rely on your advisers (primarily your accountant) to deal with the more complex matters, a basic understanding of tax laws as they pertain to charitable giving will help you to discuss knowledgeably with your accountant the charitable plan you wish to implement. Again, watch for exceptions, special rules, and future changes.

Income Tax Planning

Your donation to MJFF or any other charity will, in most cases, provide some type of income tax benefit. For many donations, maximizing your income tax charitable contribution deductions will be a key part of the planning. The following discussions review some of the many rules that will affect your deduction. Be cautious in that a host of exceptions and nuances exists for every rule discussed; these are the province of your tax advisor and well beyond the scope of this book. Don't attempt to undertake charitable planning without expert advice. Unless you're really a professional bean counter, remember the car advertisements: "Professional Driver on a Closed Course: Do Not Attempt." This maxim applies to tax planning as well.

Income Tax Deductions for Your Donations

General Requirements to Qualify for a Contribution Deduction: Charitable contributions are deducted on your personal income tax return as an itemized deduction on Schedule A, Form 1040. To be deductible, contributions must be gifts to or for the use of a qualified charitable organization, which includes MJFF. You, as the donor, must part with something of value, and the donee/charity must receive something of value. Generally, you cannot receive anything of value back from the charity in exchange for having made the donation. You must donate the entire interest in the property to qualify for a charitable contribution income tax deduction. The charity must be given full control over the cash or property you donate, and you must intend to benefit the organization in order for you to receive a tax deduction. This does not mean that you cannot specify a particular use of the funds, but the charity—not a particular individual—must benefit. While this should not prove restrictive for anyone looking to benefit the common goals of most charities serving people living with the disease, including MJFF, it would prevent you from using the organization to channel funds to a particular individual you are looking to help.

✪ EXAMPLE: Joseph Smith was touched by a single mother who lost her job as an executive secretary because her employer didn't understand or accommodate the impact her Parkinson's disease (PD) had on her ability to perform her duties. She lost her health insurance and was in severe financial need. Joseph donated $10,000 to a particular charity with the instructions that they must provide the donation as assistance to this particular woman. Although Joseph's cause and intent are admirable, he cannot use an otherwise qualified charity as a conduit to benefit a particular individual, however great the need. Joseph could donate the funds to a public charity with the non–legally binding suggestion that the charity use the donation to fund programs that would help people in similar situations, even if this particular person also benefits. The donation must be placed in the control of the charity.

✪ EXAMPLE: Chiman Lo has been a regular and substantial contributor to several charities for many years. Chiman's interests were particularly piqued by a discussion he had with an investigator researching developments in PD gene therapy research. Chiman can make a donation to the charity and direct that it be used to further this particular investigator's work, but he cannot use the organization as a conduit to benefit an individual recipient, even a researcher. MJFF, for example, will accept donations directed toward specific research projects but cannot accept donations that are restricted to supporting a particular investigator.

As illustrated throughout this book, most of the general tax rules affecting charitable contributions are replete with exceptions, exclusions, and special rules. Many of these are quite complex, and often they are not intuitive, which is why it's advisable to review the details of every charitable plan of significance with your accountant.

Donor Receives Benefit: If you realize any benefit from the property donated to charity, the amount of the charitable contribution deduction must be reduced by the value of the benefit you received. You are generally allowed to rely on an estimate of the value of any benefit provided to you by the charity. Goods or services provided to you as a donor can be ignored if they are of insubstantial value. The Internal Revenue Service (IRS) views donor benefits as insubstantial if

- The benefits you receive don't exceed the lesser of $95 or 2% of the donation.
- Your contribution is $47.50 or greater, and the only benefits are token items such as T-shirts or other items bearing the charity's name costing $9.50 or less.

Caution: Amounts change every year.

    ✪ E X A M P L E : Lynda Worthington attended a gala fund-raising dinner. The cost of the ticket was $300. Of this contribution, 2% is only $6.

She receives a gift bag of items, each of which costs the sponsoring charity $9.50 or less. Lynda's contribution will not be reduced by the value of these logo gift items, although it will be reduced by the cost of the dinner itself, of which the charity will advise her.

✪ EXAMPLE: Henritte Wolanski donated $500 to a Team Fox charitable fund-raising event in order to be listed as a sponsor in the event advertisements. She also received a special designer tote bag worth $95 for becoming a sponsor. Henritte's $500 donation does not have to be reduced by the intangible benefit she might receive by being listed as a sponsor in the advertising, but she does have to reduce her deduction by the $95 value of the tote bag.

Value of Your Contribution Deduction: The higher your marginal income tax bracket, the greater are the income tax benefits of charitable giving. If marginal income tax rates on the wealthy are increased in future years, as many expect, there may be a resulting boost in charitable giving as long as contribution deductions are not restricted. The tax benefits of charitable giving can be illustrated with a simple example.

✪ EXAMPLE: Fiona Smith donates $1,000 to charity. Fiona lives in a state that has a state income tax. Fiona's marginal federal income tax bracket is 33%, and her marginal state income tax bracket is 3.5%. The effective tax benefit is $353.45, calculated as follows: (State tax benefit is $1,000 × 3.5% = $35) + [federal tax benefit is $1,000 × 33% = $330 – ($35 state tax benefit × 33% federal rate = $11.55)]. Thus the actual out-of-pocket cost of the donation is $646.55 ($1,000 – $353.45). If Fiona's marginal federal income tax bracket is 39.6% and her marginal state income tax bracket is 3.5%, the effective tax benefit is $409.86 {(state income tax benefit of $1,000 × 3.5% = $35) + [federal tax benefit of $396 – ($35 state tax benefit × 39.6% federal rate = $13.86)]} Thus the actual out-of-pocket cost of the donation is $590.14 ($1,000 – $409.86). If Fiona is subject to the *alternative minimum tax* (AMT), the AMT rate would apply instead. Be careful of changes in these rules. The complications involved make it advisable that for any significant donations, you should have your accountant review and help you to plan the donation in advance.

Amount Deductible: When you make a cash contribution or a gift of property to or for the use of a qualified charitable organization, the amount of the cash payment, subject to the percentage limitation rules described below, is deductible unless you receive something of value in return. If you donate property to charity, the fair market value of the property, subject to the percentage limitations and other requirements outlined below, generally is deductible.

Contribution of Property That Has Not Appreciated: Donations of property that have declined in value generally are not advisable because no loss deduction will be available for the difference between the fair market value of the property and the adjusted basis of the property. Instead, you will achieve a better income tax result by selling the property and donating the net proceeds. This will permit you to deduct the loss and then claim a charitable deduction for the cash donated.

Contribution of Property That Has Appreciated: If the value of the donated property exceeds your adjusted tax basis in the property (what you paid to purchase the property plus improvements less depreciation), additional limitations and adjustments may apply depending on whether the property is real property, personal property, or tangible or intangible property. These limitations are discussed in both Chapter 4 and this chapter. Also, as noted previously, while MJFF will endeavor to accommodate and work with all donors, its preference is not to favor property donations, and it may not be able to accept such donations in all instances.

Capital Gain Property: Generally, if you donate appreciated capital gain property, you will be entitled to deduct the full fair market value of the donated property. *Capital gain property* is property that, had it been sold instead of being donated to the charity, would have generated a capital gain. However, if you deduct the entire fair market value of the property (thus avoiding tax on the appreciation if the AMT does not apply), the amount of the charitable deduction is limited to 30% of your adjusted gross income (AGI). This income limitation is explained in greater detail below. The only safe way to address possible impacts of AMT on any of your planning is to have your accountant analyze the figures under different scenarios.

Special Election to Avoid the 30% Limitation on Deduction of Appreciated Property Donation: You can avoid the preceding rule limiting your contribution deduction to 30% of your AGI if you instead agree to reduce the fair market value of the donated property by any appreciation in claiming your tax deduction. If this is done, you can then claim a deduction of up to 50% of your AGI. If the 30% limitation will apply to you and you don't have substantial appreciation in the asset involved, this election can be beneficial.

⊛ EXAMPLE: Sandra Johnson is a real estate investor. She purchased a single tract of land that she believed would appreciate when a county road project was completed. She has done nothing to improve the land. She purchased this particular lot 5 years earlier for $250,000. If she sold the lot, she, as a passive investor, would realize capital gains income. She donates the lot to charity to use for additional parking at a research center. The lot is presently valued at $320,000. Her charitable contribution deduction is $320,000. However, the amount Sandra can deduct is limited to 30% of her AGI. If, instead, Sandra attached a signed statement to her income tax return (an *election* in tax parlance) stating that she will limit her deduction by reducing the fair value of the property ($320,000) by the appreciation ($70,000) so that her deduction will be only $250,000 (which is her adjusted tax basis), the 30% AGI limitation will not apply.

Ordinary Income Property: If the property you donate to charity instead had been sold, if that sale would have generated ordinary income or a short-term capital gain, then your charitable contribution deduction is limited to the fair market value of the property reduced by the ordinary income or short-term capital gain portion. This often will be what you paid for the property.

> ✪ EXAMPLE: Mary Rhodes is a real estate developer. She purchases tracts of land, subdivides them, installs roads, sewers, and other improvements; and then sells developable lots to future homeowners. Mary is a dealer in real estate. She has a lot that she purchased 5 months earlier for $250,000, which she held for sale in the ordinary course of her business. If she sold the lot, she, as a dealer, would realize ordinary income. She donates the lot to charity to use for additional parking at a facility. The lot is presently valued at $320,000. Her charitable contribution deduction is limited to her $250,000 adjusted tax basis. If Mary had instead sold the lot, she would have paid a 40% combined federal and state income tax because capital gains treatment is not available.

Percentage Limitations on Your Charitable Contributions

Charitable contribution deductions are limited to specified percentages of your *adjusted gross income* (AGI). When planning large contributions, these limits must be considered carefully by your accountant. These rules are complex, technical, and exceedingly boring. You'll never have to be an expert in these, but an overall awareness of what the rules are about will help you to get through a charitable planning meeting with your tax adviser with a better understanding of some important restrictions on your donations. These rules get complicated, so most of the details are omitted from the following discussion.

Definition of Adjusted Gross Income: The percentage limitations are all pegged to a percentage of your AGI, which is defined as all your gross receipts (income) less certain deductions allowed under Code Section 62.

50% Limitation: There are really two 50% limitations that apply to your donations:

- All your donations in aggregate (i.e., those to all charities) cannot exceed 50% of your AGI.
- Your contributions (excluding capital gain property) to charitable organizations characterized as 50% limit organizations cannot exceed 50% of your AGI. This includes public

charities such as the MJFF, certain private operating foundations, private nonoperating foundations that make qualifying distributions of 100% of the contributions they receive within 2½ months of the close of the tax year, and certain private foundations whose contributions are pooled in a common fund and the earnings of which then are paid to public charities.

If your contributions in any year exceed the limitations, you can deduct them in any of the next five years if this limit doesn't prevent their deduction in those years. This is called a *carryover*.

30% Limitation: There are really several 30% limitations that apply to your donations:

- Deductions for your contributions to certain charities that don't qualify as 50% charities (defined earlier) are limited to 30% of your AGI. This includes contributions to veterans' organizations, fraternal societies, and certain private foundations.
- Contributions for the use of a charity are also subject to this limit. This includes, for example, a donation of an income interest in property.
- Contributions of capital gain property (when you claim a deduction for the fair market value of the property) to 50% limit organizations are limited. This occurs if you do not make the special election to reduce the contribution by the amount of appreciation, as discussed earlier.

20% Limitation: Contributions of capital gain property to organizations that do not qualify as 50% limit organizations are limited to 20% of your AGI. These are generally donations to private family foundations. This restriction does not apply to gifts to MJFF but may affect your overall planning.

Calculating the Deduction Limitation: If your contributions are subject to the percentage limitations just summarized, you'll have to use the following ordering rules to determine how those limitations apply. Thus, even if some of the preceding percentage restrictions don't apply to your donations to MJFF, they may affect your overall tax results.

- First, consider gifts to organizations that qualify for the 50% limitation.
- Next, consider contributions that are subject to the 30% limitation on non–capital gain property donated to charities that are not 50% deduction charities and donations for the use of a charity. This tier is subject to two limitations. First, all the donations in this category must be limited to 30% of your AGI. Once that is calculated, the deductions as limited cannot exceed 50% of your AGI reduced by all 50% contributions in the preceding paragraph.
- Next, the 30% limitation on capital gain property is applied. Once that is calculated, the deductions as limited cannot exceed 50% of your AGI reduced by all 50% contributions in the earlier paragraph.

- Then you can consider donations subject to the 20% limitation. Again, these are donations of capital gain assets to non-50% charities. These donations are limited to 20% of your AGI. The deduction so calculated cannot exceed 30% of your AGI reduced by the 30% of AGI contributions discussed earlier. Then the deductions as limited by all these calculations cannot exceed 50% of your AGI reduced by all 50% contributions in the earlier paragraph. Each of the percentages limitations thus is applied in a pyramid effect to the lower-tier limitations.

- The excess of your contributions in the current year over these various limitations can be deducted in (carried over to) the next 5 years subject to the same 20%, 30%, and 50% limitations.

- Contributions to veterans' organizations, nonprofit cemetery organizations, and fraternal societies subject to the 20% limit may not be carried over to future years. Thus, if you made these types of contributions, as well as a large donation to a public charity, your donation to the organization pushes you beyond 20% of your AGI, and you might lose the tax benefit of otherwise deductible contributions. Is your head spinning yet?

> ✪ EXAMPLE: Janet Williams has substantial net worth but this year only modest income. Janet's AGI is $50,000, and she resides in a state without an income tax. She donates $2,000 by check to a public charity. She also donates land with a fair market value of $30,000 to a charity. She had paid

$10,000 (adjusted tax basis) for the land. Janet donated $5,000 to a private foundation (a 30% limit organization). The following AGI limitations must be considered: Janet's 50% limit is $25,000, Janet's 30% limit is $15,000, and Janet's 20% limit is only $10,000. The result of these limitations is as follows: The cash contribution of $2,000 is allowed first. The contribution of the land is limited to 30% of the Janet's AGI, or $15,000. This generates a carryover to future years of $15,000 ($30,000 – $15,000). The $5,000 contribution to the private foundation is carried over to each of the next 5 years until used.

Itemized Deduction Rules May Limit Your Contribution Deduction

Be careful. Future tax legislation, especially efforts to raise revenues to address the growing federal deficits, may affect these rules.

Standard Deduction: You're entitled to claim certain deductions on your personal income tax return for medical expenses, tax payments, investment expenses, and so on. These deductions are collectively called *itemized deductions*. Most taxpayers do not itemize deductions because of a tax rule that lets everyone choose to deduct a set amount without any details or substantiation. This set amount, called the *standard deduction,* simplifies tax reporting for millions of taxpayers. The standard deduction in 2009 is $11,400 for joint filers and $5,700 for single filers. These amounts increase each year by an inflation adjustment (unless future tax changes modify this). If your total deductions, including charitable contributions, are less than the standard deduction, you may not realize any income tax benefit from your donation.

Most wealthy taxpayers claim itemized deductions. These are subject, of course, to limitations that may be imposed by the *alternative minimum tax* (AMT). If you itemize deductions, you might realize a full income tax benefit for the donations you make to charity. This was illustrated earlier in this chapter in an example showing the economic value of a tax deduction. However, you're not out of the tax woods just yet. A limitation exists that may affect wealthy taxpayers and reduce their deductions, including charitable contributions that otherwise would qualify as an itemized deduction.

Phaseout of Itemized Deductions: In addition to the gross income percentage limitations discussed earlier, your charitable contribution deductions may be further reduced as a result of a phaseout of itemized deductions. For income tax purposes, a charitable contribution deduction is part of your overall itemized deductions. Itemized deductions are reduced for tax years 2007 through 2009 by a percentage of your AGI. Future legislation may eliminate, extend, or expand this restriction. This phaseout is complex, and perhaps the only way to determine if it will adversely affect your contributions is to have your accountant prepare a projection of what your tax results are anticipated to be. Your itemized deductions, including contributions, are limited or reduced by the smaller of the following:

- Two percent of the excess of your AGI over a base amount. The base amount varies by year and tax filing status.
- Eighty percent of the itemized deductions you would otherwise be allowed to deduct.

Paperwork: What Documentation You Need; What You Must Report to the IRS

Paperwork is something no donor wants to deal with, but you have no choice if you want to ensure your tax benefits. The charities receiving your donations and your accountant can help you to meet the necessary requirements, so don't be deterred by them. To make the process easier for you, the following discussion is intended to help you understand some of the reporting requirements. Remember, new legislation and rules may affect these.

Documenting Cash Donated to Charity

If you donate cash to charity, your canceled check (and presumably credit-card receipt if you paid by credit card) will support your contribution deduction. Even for small cash donations, you must have a receipt from the recipient charity and/or a bank record of the contribution (canceled check).

> ✪ EXAMPLE: Jeff Johnson participated in a recent charitable fund-raising event for Team Fox. If he donated $1,000 by check mailed to the charity before the event, his canceled check will support his income tax charitable contribution deduction. However, if Jeff donated an additional $200 in cash at the event itself, he must obtain and save a receipt from MJFF to claim a tax deduction.

For cash contributions in excess of $250, the charity will report your contributions to the IRS. If you make a contribution in excess of $75, where part of the payment is a contribution and part is for goods or services (e.g., a dinner or gift item for being a sponsor), a written statement containing a good-faith estimate of the deductible portion will be provided to you. Save that letter with your tax records for the year.

> ✪ EXAMPLE: Janet Wilmington attended a fund-raising dinner for a cost of $300 per ticket. The actual value of the dinner served was $54. The charity must give Janet a written notice that only $246 is deductible.

Documenting Marketable Securities Donated

If you donate publicly traded marketable securities, no appraisal is required. If you donate securities that are not publicly traded, for example, private equity interests or interests in a family business, an appraisal is required if the claimed market value of the contribution is greater than $10,000.

Documenting Property Donated to Charity

The IRS is clearly concerned that taxpayers have abused the right to donate property (e.g., a car, art, etc.) to charities and claim a tax deduction. These rules should not dissuade you from making such donations but rather encourage you to plan such gifts carefully with your accountant so that you meet the necessary requirements. The documentation you'll need to support your tax deduction increases with the value of the donation you are making. When donations of two or more similar properties are made in the same tax year, they will be aggregated for purposes of applying this test.

Over $500, Less Than $5,000: For property donations, a reliable written record and a receipt from the recipient charity setting forth its name and other pertinent facts, such as the date and location of the contribution, are required. You'll have to provide the IRS with a detailed description of the property, the approximate date the property was acquired (if you constructed the property, the date the property was substantially completed), an explanation of how you acquired the property (e.g., gift, purchase, exchange, etc.), the fair market value of the property on the date of the donation, and a description of the method used to determine the fair market value of the property. Your accountant will have to file Form 8283, "Noncash Charitable Contributions," with your tax return.

Over $5,000, Less Than $500,000: If the value of the property contributed is greater than $5,000, the IRS requires that you obtain a qualified appraisal and file it with your income tax return. The rules for an appraisal to be qualified are pretty strict and should be carefully adhered to.

Over $500,000: The IRS may require additional reporting. Your accountant can guide you.

If the property you donated to charity was a car, boat, or airplane, additional documentation rules apply to confirm whether the organization made significant use of the property, made major repairs, or simply sold it. The IRS has sought to crack down on taxpayers donating these items and claiming deductions for values much larger than the amounts the charity receiving the property sold it for. Again, these reporting requirements should not dissuade you from donating these types of property; they simply should motivate you to have your accountant corroborate that you have the necessary documentation.

If you're a partner in a partnership or a shareholder in an S corporation that makes a property donation to charity, the partnership or corporation must comply with certain requirements. If it doesn't, you'll lose the deduction that was passed through to you to report on your personal income tax return. A partnership or S corporation also must file Form 8283 if it makes a property donation to a charity. A copy of the form must be provided to each partner or shareholder who receives an allocation of the deduction. Make sure that the entity accountant complies with the necessary reporting requirements.

Documenting Noncash Donations: Appraisal Rules

You may need to meet a number of requirements for appraisals. As with all documentation rules, these should not deter you from making property donations; rather, they should encourage you to have your accountant shepherd the process along to be sure that all the technicalities are handled properly.

An appraisal is necessary, as noted earlier, for many types of property donations. In many cases, you will have to obtain a qualified appraisal, made within a certain time, to be certain that it reflects the value at the time of your donation (not more than 60 days prior to the donation or later than the due date of your income tax return). To be a qualified appraiser, the appraiser must be a regularly practicing and paid professional (not Uncle Joe) who has not been barred from practicing before the IRS. The appraiser's compensation cannot be set as a percentage of the appraised value. The appraisal may not be provided by either the charity or the person who sold the property to you.

Penalties can be assessed if the value of donated property is overstated. The penalty is charged at a 30% rate if the amount claimed on your tax return as a deduction (the fair market value of the property or the adjusted basis) is more than 150% of the correct amount.

You cannot deduct the cost of obtaining the appraisal as a charitable contribution. The cost can be deducted as a miscellaneous itemized deduction on Schedule A, Form 1040, to the extent all miscellaneous deductions exceed 2% of your AGI. This rule will make it unlikely that you will realize a deduction for the cost of the appraisal.

Charitable Remainder Trusts

Charitable remainder trusts (CRTs) were illustrated in several examples in prior chapters. Those illustrations focused on a specific application of CRTs in the context of the examples used and did not provide an overview of CRTs. The following discussion will provide that overview to help you gain a better understanding of the technique.

Requirements for a CRT: A number of requirements must be met for a CRT to qualify for favorable tax benefits. The legal document (*trust*) that creates the CRT must state that the trust cannot be changed (*irrevocable*). The payment made from the CRT to you (and any other current recipients) must be for a term of years not in excess of 20 years or for the lives of the individual beneficiaries named (e.g., you and your spouse). The yearly payment percentage must be equal to at least 5% of the net fair market value of the trust assets. Also, the CRT cannot have a payout of greater than 50% of the fair market value of its assets. The anticipated value of the assets in the CRT when the term ends (after the specified number of years or the death of the persons named to receive payments), which will be received by charity (the *remainder interest*), determined on the date the property is contributed to the CRT, must be at least 10% of the value of the property.

> ✪ EXAMPLE: Varada and Pandu Singh want to establish a CRT. Although they want to benefit charity, they are also concerned about receiving a significant annual cash flow (annuity or unitrust payment) to support them during retirement. If the CRT is established to pay 8% per year, and Varada and Pandu are ages 55 and 54, respectively (and assuming the applicable IRS interest rate for the calculation is 5.8%), the CRT won't meet the 10% test. Effectively, the charity would be expected to get nothing when the trust terminates, based on the high 8% payout and the young ages of the two donors. If Varada and Pandu instead reduced the payout to them to 5.5%, on a $1 million donation to the CRT in 2007, they would receive $55,000 annually for the remainder of their lives. On the death of the last of Varada

and Pandu, the designated charities would be expected to receive $232,844. The 10% test is met, and the CRT will qualify for tax purposes. Varada and Pandu will be able to deduct that amount as a charitable contribution deduction on their personal income tax returns.

Types of CRTs: There are different types of CRTs, each appropriate for different donor circumstances. Many of these have been illustrated in preceding chapters. The variations in CRTs permit flexibility to use CRTs to meet a variety of donor goals:

- *Charitable remainder annuity trusts* (CRATs) provide you (or people you designate) with a fixed annuity as the current beneficiaries. Typically, the donor and the donor's spouse are named beneficiaries. However, if you wanted to name another person, such as a loved one with PD, in order to supplement his or her income, that could be done. However, the possibility of a gift tax must be planned for. The minimum payout rate from the CRAT to the donor and other named beneficiaries cannot be less than 5%. The payments to the beneficiaries are calculated based on the fair market value of the property when it is first transferred to the CRAT. Once the trust is established, no further contributions can be made to it. If the trust income is insufficient to meet the required annual return, principal must be invaded.

- *Charitable remainder unitrusts* (CRUTs) provide a form of variable annuity benefit to the current beneficiaries. The minimum rate of return to the income beneficiaries is 5%. However, unlike the CRAT, this payment is calculated based on the fair market value of the property determined on an annual basis. Thus, if the assets held by the CRUT increase in value over time, which is anticipated, a unitrust payment will grow over time. This contrasts with the payments under a CRAT, which are fixed. Thus, for a younger donor, a CRUT provides an inflation hedge to the periodic payments. The annual determination of a payment for a CRUT requires an annual appraisal, which for any property that is difficult to value (e.g., closely held business interests and real estate) could be expensive. The CRUT may provide that if the annual income earned by the trust property is insufficient to meet the required distribution to the income beneficiaries, principal may be invaded. If principal is not required to be invaded, then the trust must provide that the deficit will be made up in later years. Once a CRT in the form of a unitrust is established, additional contributions may be made in later years under certain conditions.
- *Income-only unitrusts* (NI-CRUTs) are a modified form of the CRUT. A NI-CRUT can be planned so that the current beneficiary receives an *income-only arrangement*. In a NI-CRUT, the current beneficiary would only receive the actual trust income if the income is less than the fixed percentage payment required (e.g., 5% of the trust's principal). A NI-CRUT should include its own definition of how income is to be calculated to avoid having your state laws (e.g., state principal and income acts) unintentionally affect your planning.

❂ EXAMPLE: Thomas McDonald established a NI-CRUT to benefit charity. He contributed $1 million to the trust, but the trust is *invested only in growth stocks.* The actual income earned by the NI-CRUT in the prior year was only $10,000. Even though the trust document requires a $50,000 distribution (5% × $1 million), the trust will distribute only $10,000 to Thomas.

- *Net income with a makeup unitrusts* (NIM-CRUTs) are a modified form of the NI-CRUT. A NIM-CRUT can be planned, like the NI-CRUT, so that you (as the current beneficiary) receive an income-only arrangement. But the distinguishing feature of a NIM-CRUT is that it includes a *makeup provision.* In early years, actual income may be substantially less than the 5% required CRUT payment. In later years, sufficient income may be earned to pay not only that year's payment but also to make up for some of the payments not paid in prior years. These rules were used in earlier examples that illustrated how a CRT can be planned to function effectively as a retirement plan.

❂ EXAMPLE: Daphne Hanson owns raw land worth $500,000. This land produces very modest income from an occasional rental for overflow parking to a nearby catering hall. Daphne donates this property to a NIM-CRUT that eventually will benefit various PD charities. Until the property is sold and cash is made available for income-producing investments or the property is developed to generate significant rental income, there may be little or no income. In later years, after the property is sold or made productive, when the net income of the trust exceeds the specified percentage of trust assets required to be paid (e.g., 5%), this excess then can be paid to Daphne—as the income beneficiary—to make up for the shortfall in prior years. The shortfall is determined based on the difference between the amounts actually paid in prior years, the occasional and nominal rent, and the amounts that were required to have been paid out to her based on the fixed percentage, or $25,000 per year.

- *Flip charitable remainder unitrusts* (FLIP-CRUTs) are another variation on the CRUT that provide additional planning opportunities and flexibility. In a FLIP-CRUT, you would be paid, as in the NI-CRUT, the lesser of the current income of the CRUT or the specified percentage, 5% being the minimum. When a triggering event defined in the trust document occurs, the payment method changes, or "flips," from the lesser of income or the 5% payment to a fixed percentage. A typical flip event is the sale of non-income-producing assets, such as growth stocks or raw land.

  ❂ EXAMPLE: Helen Owens inherited stock in a major company. When her mother bequeathed the stock to her, it was worth a mere $1 per share.

It is now worth $100 per share and pays almost no dividend. Helen wants to save capital gains tax on the sale, benefit charity, and secure her financial future. Helen believes that despite her PD, she'll be able to work a few more years, but not many more. When Helen stops working, the stock contributed to the FLIP-CRUT can be sold. Once the stock is sold, the trustee can invest the proceeds in income-producing assets and pay Helen a fixed percentage of that amount for the rest of Helen's life. Helen opts to use a FLIP-CRUT because until the stock is sold, the CRUT won't have any cash flow to pay her an annuity payment.

- *Inter-vivos CRTs* (of any variety) are established during your lifetime.
- *Testamentary CRTs* (of any variety) are established in your will or in another legal document and take effect on your death.

A number of other CRT permutations can further contribute to planning flexibility (and complexity!).

Income Tax Deductions of a CRT Compared with an Outright Gift of Property: If you donate property directly to any pubic charity, unless any of the special exceptions or rules discussed earlier apply, you will receive an income tax deduction for the full value of the property. And if income tax rates rise in future years, the value of this deduction will increase for contributions in those later years. However, you cannot receive anything in return other than the knowledge of having helped an important cause. If, instead, you donate property to a CRT, you (and others you name) will receive a periodic payment, possibly for life. The charity will only receive the value of the property (or what it is then invested in) after your death (or the death of you and the other named current beneficiaries). Therefore, the charitable contribution deduction will be reduced considerably with a CRT compared with an outright gift. You also need to weigh your desire to contribute currently to the charity of your choice. It might be decades before the organization receives actual dollars for programming from your CRT. This is not a reason to minimize the benefits to charity from this type of planning but to encourage you to realize that if you wish to benefit current programs, current dollars are needed in addition to CRT deferred dollars.

Income Tax Deduction on Forming a CRT: When you donate property to a CRT, you will be entitled to a deduction for income tax purposes. The deduction is based on the present value of the charitable remainder interest that charity is expected to receive when your lifetime annuity (or other) interest in the CRT ends. The amount of the charitable contribution deduction is equal to the fair market value of the property at the time of the donation to the CRT less the present value of the income interest retained by you (or by you and your spouse, if a named beneficiary). The value of the income tax deduction to you will depend on numerous factors, including your marginal tax bracket (the higher the better—remember, capital gains are presently being taxed at historically low rates), the income interest reserved to you and perhaps others (the greater the income interest, the lower is the tax deduction), the applicability of the charitable contribution limitations discussed earlier, and other factors.

Gift and Estate Tax Consequences of a CRT: Although the focus of this section is on income tax planning for your charitable contribution deductions, a brief note on the estate and gift tax implications of your CRT is worthwhile. In addition to the current income tax deduction, you may also receive a valuable estate tax benefit as well. If you are one of the income beneficiaries of the charitable trust, the value of the trust will be included in your gross estate when you die. However, since the interest will pass to a qualified charity, an offsetting estate tax charitable contribution deduction occurs. Thus the value of the property donated effectively will be removed from your estate.

How Beneficiaries Are Taxed on CRT Distributions: The amount paid to a beneficiary (the donor and his or her spouse) under a CRT retains the character that the property had inside the trust. Some donors mistakenly believe that the only income tax consequence of the CRT is their current income tax deduction, but this is not the full story. The distributions from the CRT have an income tax consequence to you and any other recipients:

- You and the other beneficiaries report a portion of each year's CRT distributions as ordinary income, to the extent of the CRT's current and prior undistributed income.

- After all ordinary income is exhausted, amounts then will be taxed as a short-term capital gain, to the extent of current and past undistributed short-term capital gains.
- Next, distributions from the CRT are taxed as long-term capital gain, to the extent of current and past undistributed long-term capital gains.
- Then distributions are taxed as other income, such as tax-exempt income, to the extent of the trust's current and past undistributed income of such character.
- Finally, any further distributions are treated as tax-free distributions of principal.

The trust itself generally will be exempt from tax. Thus a CRT can sell the appreciated property that you gift to it without incurring any gain (but, as discussed earlier, that gain is recognized by you as distributions are received by you from the trust). However, if the trust generates *unrelated business taxable income* (UBTI), it can be subject to tax. This can be an issue when trust assets are debt financed, stock in an active business is contributed to the trust, or other special circumstances occur. These rules are extremely complex and require professional assistance.

Gift Tax Planning

Overview of the Gift Tax

The gift tax is assessed on transfers you make to people during your lifetime. The most common example of gift tax rules, which you are likely to be familiar with, is that you can gift away $13,000 in any year to any person with no gift tax implications. This is called the *gift tax annual exclusion*. This amount will be adjusted in future years for inflation. In addition to the gift tax annual exclusion, which you can gift to as many people as you wish, you can gift $1 million in aggregate during your lifetime. After both these amounts are exceeded, a gift tax will apply to tax the value of any assets you give away. There has been some talk about Congress unifying the gift and estate taxes. If this occurred, it might increase the gift exclusion to the current $3.5 million estate exclusion or take some other form, if it happens at all.

Gift Tax Charitable Contribution Deduction

When you make gifts to charities in excess of the $13,000 per year gift tax exclusion, you will face a gift tax consequence unless the gift is to a qualifying charity, which includes MJFF. In such cases, you may qualify for an unlimited gift tax charitable contribution deduction.

Using Charitable Lead Trusts to Minimize Gift Tax Consequences

As illustrated in earlier chapters, a *charitable lead trust* (CLT) can be used in many creative ways to benefit charity and achieve several important personal goals. This discussion provides a more detailed explanation of the CLT technique, although many aspects remain beyond the scope of this brief discussion.

Overview of CLTs: Although the CLT technique can be used to minimize estate taxes (and can be quite useful in that regard), it is discussed here in the context of minimizing gift taxes on lifetime transfers. A CLT is also called a *front trust* because the charitable beneficiary receives its income before, or in "front of," the ultimate beneficiaries (remainder beneficiaries) receiving their share. Typically, the remainder beneficiaries are your children, although other beneficiaries can be named. The CLT can be a valuable and appropriate estate planning tool when you have (1) charitable intent, (2) the desire to increase the eventual (but not current) net worth of family members or other designated heirs, and (3) the goal of reducing gift and estate taxes. A significant CLT benefit is that appreciation after assets are transferred to the CLT ultimately will pass to your beneficiaries free of any gift or estate tax.

Gift Tax Benefits of a CLT: There are many benefits and reasons for setting up a CLT. CLTs can be significant in reducing gift or estate tax cost. The reduction in tax cost is achieved by virtue of the fact that the remainder beneficiaries must wait to receive the property until expiration of the charitable beneficiary's interest. The concept can be illustrated with a simple example.

> ✪ E X A M P L E : Ignatius Koutourdias gives $600,000 to a CLT. A named charity will receive annual payments (usually in the form of an annuity or unitrust amount) for each year of the CLT. The end of the trust will occur after the number of years Ignatius determined when setting up the trust.

Assuming Ignatius selected a 22-year term for the CLT, Ignatius' children will receive the trust assets (this hopefully will be substantially more than $600,000 depending on the investment results during the period the charity received payments). If the term of the charitable interest is made long enough, the value of the gift Ignatius made to his children can be reduced to nearly zero for purposes of the gift tax.

✿ E X A M P L E : Michael O'Connor gifts $500,000 to a CLT for a 25-year term in 2007. A charity is designated to receive annual payments of $30,000 (at a 6% rate) each year for 20 years. Following the end of the CLT in year 25, Michael's children will receive the trust assets. With a 6% payout and professional investment management, Michael anticipates that the payment will be substantially more than the $500,000 initial gift. For gift tax purposes, the value of the future gift to Michael's children is reduced from $500,000 to about $100,000. At a 50% estimated tax rate, the savings could be $200,000.

Charitable and Personal Benefits of a CLT: You can meet long-term charitable giving objectives using a CLT. Establishing a CLT will ensure the annual distributions of a specified amount (where an annuity arrangement is used) to a charity for a specified number of years.

✪ EXAMPLE: Wendy Bochamp has been actively involved with MJFF and likes the idea of funding specific projects to ensure their success. She establishes a 20-year CLT for her son, Fernando, who has PD, that will benefit MJFF during the interim 20 years. She plans on funding the CLT with $700,000. If the payout rate is 5%, the organization will receive $35,000 per year for 20 years. Wendy arranges an agreement with MJFF so that her son can approve which projects these funds will be used for. This approach enables Fernando to stay actively involved. The plan also will provide significant gift tax benefit to Wendy and gives MJFF assurance that a series of programs in future years will be funded as a result of Wendy's generosity. Wendy can designate in the agreement with MJFF that in the event Fernando resigns or becomes unable to remain involved, she will recommend the annual gifts. Wendy feels that as long as her son has the ability and interest, he should have the option whether to work with MJFF on disbursement of funds so that he can play an active role is research so vital to his future. Wendy preferred this approach to using a private foundation because she feels that she can accomplish the same charitable and educational goals but will give her son, who lives with PD, an opportunity to be actively involved with MJFF *and* a financial safety net in 20 years. It's Wendy's hope that if her son has adequate assets when the CLT ends, he'll simply donate the entire trust balance to MJFF. Wendy writes a personal letter of instruction to be given to her son when the trust ends to encourage this.

Using a CLT to Time Distributions to Heirs: You can defer and control when your heirs receive funds by timing the termination of the CLT to coincide with different events or milestones (e.g., a beneficiary attaining age 65). This was illustrated in earlier chapters showing how to use a CLT to create a retirement plan for a partner or child. The duration for which a CLT lasts can be coordinated with other estate and financial planning to ensure the availability of assets for a long-term time horizon for your children or other heirs.

✪ EXAMPLE: Tina Fergenti establishes a trust under her will to pay income annually to her child. Principal is to be paid out of the trust fund in approximately one-third equal amounts when the child attains the ages of 30, 35, and 40 years. The child is presently age 22. If Tina establishes a CLT for a duration of 23 years [(40 − 22) + 5], the child will receive the assets of the CLT at age 45. This is timed to continue the five-year payment sequence with the hope of distributing assets in stages to both protect the remaining assets and to minimize the potentially adverse consequences of the child receiving too much wealth at one time.

Drawbacks of Using a CLT: Tax and other benefits can be realized only if the CLT meets all applicable tax law requirements, which can be burdensome, costly, and difficult. For example, CLTs can be subject to the rules applicable to private foundations concerning self-dealing, excess business holdings, jeopardy investments, and the like. A special tax is imposed on a CLT that sells or exchanges property within 2 years of the date when the property was transferred to the CLT. When this rule applies, the CLT is taxed at your income tax rate. The objective of this provision is to prevent you from gaining a tax advantage by transferring property intended for sale to a CLT to sell. CLTs are not tax-exempt. A CLT only avoids taxation if the amounts paid to charity are sufficient to offset any income tax otherwise due by the CLT. Gifts to CLTs do not qualify for the gift tax annual exclusion. CLTs create complications for *generation-skipping transfer* (GST) *tax* planning. The GST exclusion cannot be allocated to a CLT until the charitable interest ends. Thus, if a 20-year CLAT is used, the determination will be made at the end of year 20. If the CLT works as planned, this is when the assets will be highly appreciated and the allocation most inefficient to make. The better option is to use a CLUT because the allocation of the GST tax amount can be made when you set up the CLT initially.

Types of CLTs: Your CLT can be prepared in a manner that will qualify it so that all the CLT income is taxed to you (a *grantor trust*) or so that the CLT pays its own income tax and files its own tax return (a *nongrantor trust*). In either event, two points warrant your attention. A CLT is never a tax-free entity like the CRT discussed earlier. Because the CLT is not a tax-exempt entity, a deduction will be created each year as the CLT makes its annual donation to charity. This charitable contribution deduction would be used to offset your income if your CLT is planned as a grantor trust or the trust's income if it is not. A CLT often is structured as a nongrantor trust. This means that CLT earnings are not taxed to you. You will not receive an income tax deduction for any charitable contributions made by the CLT during its term. If, instead, the CLT is structured to be a grantor trust, you will be taxed on the income earned by the trust (unless the income is primarily tax-exempt bond income). However, you also will qualify for deductions for the charitable contributions made by the CLT.

Estate Tax Planning

Charitable Bequests Under Your Will: Trusts

Charitable planning can be integrated into your estate planning to accomplish personal, tax, and other goals. You can make direct bequests to a charity in your will. Many people opt to make bequests in their wills not only to benefit a particular charitable cause but also to demonstrate to their children and other heirs the importance of making a contribution back to society by benefiting charities. You can create trusts to benefit family or other beneficiaries who also might benefit charity. Apart from these rather simple approaches that encompass charitable giving, a number of more complex charitable giving techniques use charitable gifts. Many of these were discussed in Chapters 3 through 5, and some are noted again here.

Taxable Versus Probate Estate

Many people confuse the concepts of *taxable estate* and *probate estate*. Your taxable estate is comprised of the assets in which you had sufficient interests on your death that the tax laws deem those assets owned by you for purposes of assessing an estate tax. Your probate estate are the assets passing under your will—that is, through the probate- or court-administered process of administering your estate. Many assets that are not part of your probate estate still may be included in your taxable estate. For example, insurance on your life that you owned or for which you retained significant rights (*incidence of ownership*) is not part of your probate estate but is included in your taxable estate. This can be important to understand in planning the magnitude of charitable gifts you wish to provide for in your will or other estate planning documents. Your taxable estate may be much larger than your probate estate, and you may have a greater potential estate tax liability than you anticipate. The distinction between your taxable and probate estate is important if you anticipate giving a certain portion of your estate to charity.

Estate Tax Charitable Contribution Deduction

Your estate is entitled to deduct any donations made to charity for property included in your estate if these donations are given to a qualified charity.

Estate Tax Allocation Clause

If your estate must pay estate taxes, those taxes must be paid from some designated portion of your estate. The provision in your will that designates which bequests and which assets are to be used to pay estate taxes is called the *tax-allocation clause*. This provision is too often overlooked or dismissed as standard (*boilerplate*). This can be a costly mistake that undermines your charitable and other planning. The tax-allocation clause should be reviewed carefully and tailored to meet the specific goals you have for your estate. In most cases, if you make a bequest to charity, you don't want any portion of that otherwise deductible charitable bequest used toward an estate tax liability. If you do, then the portion of the estate tax paid from the bequest to charity will reduce that bequest, perhaps undermining your charitable goals. It also will create a spoiler effect in that the dollars used to pay tax instead would have gone to charity, thus reducing your charitable deduction and, in turn, increasing the tax owed. If you have a trust that can benefit both family and charity, the decision as to how taxes should be allocated is not as clear.

Using Charitable Planning to Minimize Estate Taxes

The CLT discussed earlier, in the context of gift tax planning, also can be used to minimize your estate tax. A *testamentary* (after your death) CLT can be formed under your will.

✿ E X A M P L E : Melinda Boyle's estate is valued at $5 million. She understands that the estate tax exclusion, presently $3.5 million for federal tax purposes, but only $1 million for state estate tax purposes, will leave her with a taxable estate. She is reluctant to complicate her life with involved estate tax planning techniques while she is alive, but she isn't fond of the idea of paying a significant estate tax either. As an initial measure, until she decides to undertake more complex planning, she includes a $1 million CLT in her will that substantially reduces any potential federal estate tax on the value of her estate in excess of the current $3.5 million exclusion. If the law changes, she'll only have to modify or delete that bequest in her will. If it doesn't change, she'll have saved estate tax with no current hassles. If there is an estate tax, charity will receive the benefit in lieu of the IRS. Melinda is rather pleased with the tradeoff.

Will You Realize Estate Tax Benefits from Your Donation?

Charitable gifts from your estate can be beneficial from personal and charitable perspectives regardless of the estate tax benefit. However, if your charitable planning is based on the realization of estate tax savings, you should be realistic about what those savings may be.

Properly structured, high-value charitable gifts can reduce potential estate taxes significantly. This can help to address potential estate liquidity problems, thus increasing flexibility to retain relatively nonliquid business or real estate interests. The estate tax benefits of charitable giving similarly will depend on your combined federal and state estate tax liability (or just state if your estate is below the federal exemption amount, which is $3.5 million in 2009). Since the estate tax exemption was increased from $600,000 years ago to $3.5 million in 2009, fewer donors benefit from federal estate tax charitable deductions. However, many states have much lower thresholds for estate taxation, and donors in high estate-tax states will continue to realize state estate tax benefits for much smaller estates.

Chapter Summary

If any of the techniques discussed in Chapters 1 through 5 of this book interest you, you should review the more detailed rules that affect the techniques in this chapter. This chapter discussed many of the more technical aspects of charitable giving, especially the rules for income tax deduction for charitable contributions. The income tax deduction rules are detailed and important because they will affect how you structure almost any charitable plan to benefit charity and achieve your other goals. The goal of this chapter was to provide you with a general understanding of some of the important issues involved. However, the myriad exceptions and special rules and the likelihood of new tax developments make it essential that you review these matters with your professional advisers before implementing any plan.

CHAPTER SEVEN

WHAT YOU CAN DO NEXT

H OPEFULLY, YOU'VE DOG-EARED at least of couple of pages containing ideas that caught your attention. The goal of this chapter is to help you turn those dog-ears into action—action that will benefit people and goals you care about, action that will benefit charities, perhaps The Michael J. Fox Foundation (MJFF) among them.

Identify the People, Assets, and Goals You're Concerned About

The first step in your planning process is to identify the people you are concerned about, the assets you have to work with, and the goals you have. No planning really can be undertaken without this essential personal input.

People: Identify all the people in your immediate family, whether you wish to provide for them, and if so, to what extent. Identify any people who are not relatives and the extent to which you wish to provide for them. Background information on each of these people is important to note so that your professional advisers and charitable giving professionals from the charities you will benefit all can work together to make sure that these people are provided for. For example, if you have a child who is quite well-to-do, a *charitable lead trust* (CLT) that will benefit him in the future may be a great technique. If you have another child who is living with the challenges of young-onset Parkinson's disease (PD) and unable to work, a trust that will provide benefit in 20 years will be, practically speaking, useless. On the other hand, a *charitable remainder trust* (CRT) that benefits the latter child immediately and ensures a quarterly payment for life might be ideal. You must document key details on the people who are important to you so that your planning can be tailored accordingly. Don't assume that your adviser will know the circumstances of the people who are important to you. If you or a loved one has PD, you should be diligent to explain to all your advisers the current circumstances and anticipated disease course so that they can help you to plan appropriately. If your advisers are not personally familiar with PD, however capable and well-meaning, they may misunderstand the implications.

Assets: Prepare (or have your financial planner or accountant prepare or work with you on) a balance sheet listing all your assets and liabilities. It is essential for your advisers to understand the assets you have in order to identify the appropriate planning techniques. If your house is a unique beachfront property that has been in your family for generations, a plan that would transfer ownership to charity, while tax advantageous, might be contrary to one of your key objectives. If your balance sheet reflects liquidity problems, then increasing your liquidity should be a focus of your planning. The assets you own, as well as their specific characteristics and how they fit into your overall financial picture, are all essential facts needed to develop an optimal plan.

Goals: Two people with identical family relationships and assets might have dramatically different plans. The differences are due to the varying goals that people in otherwise similar situations may have. The more clearly and specifically you can elucidate your financial, estate, tax, business, retirement, and personal goals, the better those goals will be achieved. Write them down. Be clear.

Working with Your Advisers

You can't develop, implement, or monitor any charitable giving plan without the coordination of all your advisers. The ideal method of accomplishing this is to have all your key advisers meet to review a proposed plan, but this can be impractical because of costs and scheduling. In most cases, the coordination you need among multiple advisers can be accomplished with a few simple conference calls. You might, for example, meet at your attorney's office with a charity's major- or planned-gift professional and make a conference call to your accountant and wealth manager at the appropriate points in the meeting. The key is to involve the necessary advisers and be sure that they communicate so that your plan will be developed in the most advantageous way and, once developed, will be implemented and monitored to ensure your success.

Your advisers could include:

Accountant: Your accountant will have to help review and address the income, gift, and estate tax consequences of any plan you are considering. In most cases, it will be advisable for your accountant to complete projections of the anticipated tax result from any plan.

These projections can identify traps or opportunities to tailor your plan to better fit your goals. For example, if you're planning a CRT, some strict tests must be met. These requirements should be reviewed in advance of consummating a plan. Once your plan is decided on, your accountant may have a role in completing financial information, analyzing tax matters, and dealing with other issues. After your plan is implemented, your accountant will have a key role in maintaining and operating your plan. This will include the preparation of any necessary income tax returns.

Financial Planner or Wealth Manager: A key to many of the planning techniques reviewed in this book is investment performance. For example, if you establish a CLT to benefit your child with YO PD in 20 years, the growth of that portfolio at a rate greater than the payments to charity during the 20-year term will ensure a substantial retirement plan and safety net. Investment performance must be tailored to the plan. CRTs are tax-exempt; CLTs are not. Different plans require different investment approaches (asset locations) and rates of return and have different cash-flow needs.

Insurance Consultant: If you donate large assets directly to charity or to a CRT to benefit charity, you might wish to use life insurance to replace the value of the assets your heirs won't receive as a result of the donation. If you engage in any type of charitable planning, you might wish to use insurance to protect family or other potential heirs. Insurance is also a powerful charitable giving technique. You can gift a policy you no longer need, have a new policy purchased, or engage in other types of insurance planning to benefit charity. In all these cases, the input of your insurance consultant to select the optimal insurance product to achieve your goals is vital to the success of your plan. Once your plan is selected, your insurance consultant will be needed to help implement the plan. This may include insurance applications, changing beneficiaries or owners of policies, and other matters. If you gift substantial assets, your need for disability or long-term care insurance may have to be reevaluated. Once your plan is implemented, your insurance consultant will have to be involved periodically to monitor the plan.

Pension Adviser: If you plan to gift or bequeath any portion of your retirement assets to charity, you will need the assistance of your pension adviser.

Attorney: Your attorney must review any legal issues involved in your proposed plan. For example, if your plan involves buying an insurance policy for charity, your attorney should confirm that there is no issue of the named charity having an insurable interest so that they can in fact own the policy. Every plan requires that legal documents be drafted. It's not only the specific trust that may be the focal point of your charitable plan, such as a CRT, but also all the ancillary documents. If you establish a CRT, your will might include specific provisions relating to that CRT. If you make a bequest in your will of a specific asset to charity, your attorney will have to draft that language in your will. Your attorney may choose to also modify your durable power of attorney to prevent your agent from making a change or transfer of the asset you've bequeathed to charity in your will.

Major Gift or Planned Giving Professional: If you're planning a significant current or planned gift to charity, a major-gift or planned-gift professional is an essential part of your planning team. If you're purchasing or donating assets for a gift annuity, you'll need guidance on what is available. If you're funding a specific project or series of projects, the charity will help you to draft the language of a donor agreement so that your contribution will accomplish the most good. If you want to involve your donee or heir who has PD in the planned-giving process, charitable professionals can show you how to accomplish this. Once your plan is conceived, implementation will involve your charitable professional coordinating those matters affecting the organization. Once your plan is implemented, depending on the plan, there may be little ongoing involvement from the charity until the gift or bequest is received. In some instances, however, such as a CLT paying an annuity every year, you'll want ongoing contact with your planned-giving professional.

Develop a Comprehensive Plan

One-dimensional plans don't work. Plans that focus on a single "magic bullet" or technique don't work. Life is complex and full of uncertainty, and any charitable giving plan you decide on, other than a simple donation that is not a significant portion of your wealth, will succeed only if it is part of an integrated overall estate, tax, retirement, and financial plan. Your plan should include and coordinate:

Estate Planning Documents: At minimum, you will need four key documents in your plan. These are (1) a durable power of attorney (authorizes an agent to handle tax, legal, and financial matters), (2) a health care proxy (designates an agent to make health care decisions for you), (3) a living will (a statement of your health care wishes), and (4) a will (distributes assets, appoints guardians, etc.). Depending on the nature of your plan, you may require a range of different trusts such as a revocable living trust, insurance trust, charitable remainder trust (CRT), charitable lead trust (CLT), marital trust (QTIP), and so on.

Investment Plan: You should have an overall investment-allocation plan for all your assets. Within that plan, each separate investment basket (asset location) must be planned. Your tax-deferred accounts, such as individual retirement accounts (IRAs), may have different investment allocations than a bypass trust under your late husband's will. If you establish a charitable trust, its assets will have to be planned with appropriate consideration to the trust terms.

Life and Related Insurance: Your insurance needs, which could include life insurance, disability insurance, and long-term care insurance, should be evaluated based on your circumstances and the planning you pursue. If you donate significant assets to charity, you might feel more inclined to opt for long-term care insurance than you may have been had you retained full control over a larger asset base.

Property and Casualty Insurance: You must be certain that all property, fire, casualty, and other risks are properly addressed. This coverage is essential to protect the assets you retain. Further, insurance coverage will often have to be modified as you implement your plan. If you give commercial real estate to a CRT, that trust and its trustees should be listed as named insureds on the property and casualty insurance. Your umbrella or personal excess liability coverage must be coordinated with the ownership and size of your assets.

Tax Returns and Planning: Your accountant should be certain that all applicable tax returns (i.e., income, gift, estate, etc.) are filed. Ongoing tax planning often will be required to address changes in facts or the law.

Implement Your Plan

So now you've identified the people, assets, and goals that are important to you. You have developed a comprehensive plan with an integrated planning team—it's time to pull the trigger and implement your plan. Too often the excitement and motivation are lost when you reach the implementation stage of a plan. Don't lose sight of the end goal. It's vital that you continue your focus on implementation of your plan. You need to follow up with all your advisers to be certain that they are all in agreement with the plan and understand their respective roles. Regardless of the roles you believe any of your advisers are taking, you should be certain that all aspects of your plan are implemented, all documents signed, all accounts opened, and all other issues are dealt with.

Monitor Your Plan

Most charitable planning techniques will require periodic monitoring to ensure that they are being handled properly. The following is a partial checklist for many of the techniques noted in this book. However, you should assemble your own personalized checklist with your advisers for your exact plan.

Bequest Under Your Will

If you make a bequest in your will to one or more charities, that bequest should be monitored periodically. The following are some of the possible steps you should review with your advisers:

- The charities should be properly named in full, including the state and city in which they're located.
- The charities should be notified of the bequest.
- The charities should review the language to be certain that it will achieve your intended goal.

- You should sign a pledge agreement confirming and backing up the bequest. This can be important for a bequest paid over time so that in the event of your disability or demise, your agents and executors will be aware of your commitment and to provide them with the legal authority to pay an remaining installments (if the commitment is binding). If the charity makes commitments to you as to what your donations will be used for, this should be documented, with options if circumstances change.
- Your overall financial and estate plan should be reviewed annually to be certain that the size of the bequest is consistent with your current goals, net worth, and other factors.
- If your bequest was specific as to the application of the dollars to be given, such as for a specific research goal, you must confirm that the narrowness is still appropriate in light of new developments. PD research is dynamic. It would be unfortunate to create legal entanglements by leaving a bequest for a specific type of research that is no longer relevant.

Charitable Lead Trust

A CLT provides a distribution during its term to your chosen charities, and thereafter, funds are distributed to your designated heirs. The following are some of the monitoring steps that you should review with your advisers:

- Your advisers must determine whether the trust is to be taxed as a grantor trust or a non-grantor trust, and the trust and plan must be tailored accordingly.

- The trust document creating the CLT must be properly signed.
- A tax identification number (TIN) must be obtained from the Internal Revenue Service (IRS).
- Assets you've identified for contribution to the CLT must be transferred.
- CLT assets must be invested in a manner that comports with the goals of your plan.
- Your accountant must file an annual tax return (the type of which will depend on the manner in which your CLT was planned).
- If your CLT is a *charitable lead unitrust* (CLUT), the trust assets must be valued each year.
- Periodic distributions to your chosen charities (at least annually but perhaps more frequently) must be made as required in the CLT.
- Depending on your agreement with the charities, there may be involvement with major-gift professionals each year as to the use of the funds being donated.
- Investment performance must be monitored.
- Annual records of all trust activities must be kept by the trustee.
- Depending on the terms of the trust document and state law, the trustees may have certain reporting obligations to the beneficiaries.
- When the trust term ends, the assets must be distributed to your heirs (or in many cases to further trusts to protect them), the trust agreement must terminate, a final tax return must be filed, and other housekeeping actions must be taken.

Charitable Remainder Trust

A CRT provides a distribution during its term to you and possibly to other named beneficiaries. After the trust term has ended, the named charities receive the trust assets. You will obtain an income tax deduction on the donation to the CRT. The following are some of the monitoring steps that you should review with your advisers:

- The trust document creating the CRT must be properly signed. Your advisers must verify that the 50%, 10%, and other tests discussed in Chapter 6 are met.
- A tax identification number (TIN) must be obtained from the IRS.
- Assets you've identified for contribution to the CRT must be transferred.
- Any unique nuances of those assets must be considered and planned for. For example, if you transfer real estate to a CRT, the trustees and/or charitable beneficiary may require a title report, environmental inspection, and other steps to protect the CRT. Property and casualty insurance must be amended to list the trust and trustees as named insureds.
- If you've also paired your CRT with an insurance plan to replace assets for your heirs, that plan must be monitored separately.
- CRT assets must be invested in a manner that comports with the goals of your plan.
- Your accountant must file an annual tax return.

- If your CRT is a *charitable remainder unitrust* (CRUT), the trust assets must be valued each year.
- Periodic distributions to the current beneficiaries (at least annually but perhaps more frequently) must be made as required in the CRT.
- Investment performance must be monitored.
- Any unique nuances of your CRT must be monitored. If the trust is structured as a FLIP-CRUT, the event that triggers the flip in payments must be monitored. If your CRT is structured as a NIM-CRUT, as explained in Chapter 6, the makeup payments must be monitored.
- Annual records of all trust activities must be kept by the trustee.
- Depending on the terms of the trust document and state law, the trustees may have certain reporting obligations to the beneficiaries.
- When the trust term ends, the assets must be distributed to the named charities, the trust agreement must terminate, a final tax return must be filed, and other housekeeping actions must be taken.

Donating Insurance to Charity

You can use insurance in a host of ways in your charitable plan. The simplest is to donate an insurance policy to charity. The following are some of the monitoring steps that you should review with your advisers if you are using an insurance trust in your plan:

- Have your attorney confirm that, under your state law, the named charities will have the legal right to own insurance on your life (*insurable interest*).
- Review available insurance products with your insurance consultant and major-gift professional from the recipient charities.
- Apply for a permanent insurance policy to be owned by the charities.
- Contribute cash as a donation each year to the charities so that the organizations can purchase the policy.
- If you are transferring an existing policy to the trust, it must be valued and all necessary assignment documents completed and filed with the insurance company issuing the policy.
- Insurance performance must be monitored. This might mean obtaining an in-force policy illustration periodially and checking on the financial status of the insurance company.

Irrevocable Life Insurance Trust

Another way to use insurance in your charitable plan is to establish an *irrevocable life insurance trust* (ILIT) to own insurance on your life to replace assets you've given to charity. You can simply donate a policy to charity or engage in other types of insurance and charitable planning discussed in this book. The checklist to monitor each of these plans will be quite different depending on the nature of your plan. The following are some of the general monitoring steps that you should review with your advisers if you are using an insurance trust in your plan:

- The insurance trust document, if one is to be used, must be properly signed.
- A tax identification number (TIN) must be obtained from the IRS.
- Contribute cash at inception and usually annually thereafter to the trust to pay for insurance premiums.
- If you are transferring an existing policy to the trust, it must be valued and all necessary assignment documents completed and filed with the insurance company issuing the policy.
- Annual demand or "crummey" power notices must be issued by your trustees to the beneficiaries in order to qualify annual gifts to the trust for the annual gift tax exclusion. Discuss this planning step with your advisers.
- Trust assets must be invested in a manner that comports with the goals of your plan. In most cases, this will be a modest amount of cash maintained in a non-interest-bearing checking account.
- Insurance performance must be monitored. This might mean obtaining an in-force policy illustration periodically and checking on the financial status of the insurance company.
- Annual records of all trust activities must be kept by the trustee.
- Depending on the terms of the trust document and state law, the trustees may have certain reporting obligations to the beneficiaries.

- When the trust term ends, the assets must be distributed to the named charities and perhaps any other beneficiaries, the trust agreement must terminate, a final tax return must be filed, and other housekeeping actions must be taken.

Monitor Your Overall Plan, Not Just One Charitable Technique

During all phases of your planning, you must be sure that each key person you've identified is protected, that assets you have are integrated into the plan in the most optimal manner, and that your plan is monitored on a regular basis to ensure that it remains on track to meet your goals. The entire process is dynamic. The people you are concerned about protecting may change over time. The circumstances affecting each of them certainly will change over time. Your assets will change. Even your goals may change as you age, mature, and new situations and circumstances evolve. A diagnosis of PD changes so many aspects of your life. Your planning must be monitored for these changes as well as the formalities listed here.

Chapter Summary

The techniques or planning ideas in this book that caught your attention were developed into components of a comprehensive plan in this chapter. Checklists and practical suggestions about how develop you own action plan help you to take the next step.

This chapter explained the practical and detailed follow-up you need to really make any charitable plan work for you. Without the proper follow-up, your plan is unlikely to achieve your many personal goals.

Now that you have the ideas and action steps to take, make up your own checklist of to-do items, follow up with your advisers, and begin the process of supporting your chosen charity while achieving other important personal goals.

GLOSSARY

Adjusted gross income (AGI): Total earnings (wages, interest, dividends, rental income, etc.) of a donor reported on Form 1040, "Personal Income Tax Return," reduced only by certain limited deductions (e.g., alimony, IRA contributions, etc.). AGI is the benchmark for determining when limitations are applied to deducting certain charitable contributions.

Alternative minimum tax (AMT): A tax calculation that limits deductions and other preferential tax benefits and may result in all your income being taxed at a flat rate that is lower than the regular tax but with a resulting higher tax. This might result in a lower income tax benefit from a charitable gift.

Annual exclusion: The amount that anyone can gift each year to another (other than a charity) without incurring any gift tax consequences.

Appraisal: Donations of property to charity must be supported by a formal determination of value (appraisal) that meets specified requirements of the tax laws.

Benefit: If you receive a valuable benefit that is more than a token gift (e.g., a dinner) in recognition of your donation, the amount of your charitable contribution deduction may have to be reduced.

Carry forward: If you cannot use a current contribution as a deduction in the current year because of limitations on your contribution deduction, you may be able to claim the unused deductions in future years.

Charitable bailout: In some instances, you might be able to donate stock in a closely held business or real estate venture to charity directly or to a charitable remainder trust (CRT), obtain a current income tax deduction, and provide a mechanism for succession planning of the business or venture.

Charitable lead annuity trust: A trust that pays a fixed annuity amount in each year of its term to charity, following which the assets of the trust are distributed to heirs of the donor, usually children.

Charitable lead unitrust: A trust that pays a variable amount determined each year based on the asset value of the trust to charity, following which the assets of the trust are distributed to the heirs of the donor, which may include children or even grandchildren.

Charitable remainder annuity trust: A trust that pays a fixed percentage of the initial value of assets contributed to the trust for a specified number of years or for life. Following these interests, named charities receive the assets.

Charitable remainder unitrust: A charitable trust that pays the donor a variable amount each year based on a fixed percentage (determined when the trust is established) of the value of the trust assets each year.

Child: You can benefit a child and charity using charitable lead trusts (CLTs), making a child a current beneficiary of a charitable remainder trust (CRT) with you and using other techniques.

Closely held business: A number of charitable giving techniques can benefit a closely held or family business, including donations of inventory, donations that are deductible without limitation as advertising expenses, charitable bailouts of stock, and more.

Depreciation: The systematic deduction of the portion of the cost of building and acquiring an asset, such as a building, over a period allowed by the tax laws. If depreciable assets are donated to charity, a portion of the deduction may be reduced based on prior depreciation deductions.

Estate tax: A tax assessed on the value of assets and certain other rights you own at death. Outright contributions to charity are deductible in full against the amounts subject to tax.

Fair market value: The value a willing buyer would pay to a willing seller with full knowledge of the transaction. While many types of donations to charity are deductible based on the fair market value of assets you donate, other deductions are limited.

Farm: You can donate a remainder interest in a farm. You can use or live in it for your lifetime (and your spouse's if you wish), and on death, the property will be transferred to charity.

Generation-skipping transfer (GST) tax: A tax that applies, in addition to the gift and estate taxes, to multigenerational transfers made to generations below that of a donor's children, such as grandchildren.

Gift annuity: A donor gifts property, such as appreciated stock, to The Michael J. Fox Foundation (MJFF) in exchange for specified periodic payments for life. Also called a *charitable gift annuity* (CGA).

Gift tax: A tax is assessed on the lifetime transfer of assets. The first $12,000 per person is excluded from gift tax (this amount is inflation adjusted), and you can gift $1 million before incurring tax. Charitable giving techniques that benefit desired charities can be used to minimize gift tax impact on large transfers to your heirs.

Grandchild: Gifts or bequests to grandchildren can trigger the generation-skipping transfer (GST) tax. Incorporating charitable giving into your planning for grandchildren (and even further descendants) can enable you to minimize the GST tax impact.

Inter-vivos: A gift made while the donor is alive is referred to as an inter-vivos gift.

Inventory: Businesses can donate inventory items to charity and obtain valuable tax deductions.

IRA: You can bequeath your individual retirement account (IRA) or other retirement plan accounts to charity and save substantial income and estate taxes. A limited opportunity exists to donate up to $100,000 of your IRA to charity while you are alive.

Itemized deductions: You are allowed to deduct a list of possible expenditures, including charitable contributions, as deductions on your personal income tax return. The limitations on these deductions may affect the value of your charitable contribution deductions.

Life insurance donations: You can donate existing insurance policies or buy a new policy for a designated charity.

Life insurance replacement: You can purchase life insurance to replace the value of the assets you donate to charity so that your estate stays whole.

Mortgaged property: If you donate mortgaged property to charity, you will have an income tax consequence.

Part gift/part sale: If a donor sells an asset at a reduced favorable price to charity, the bargain portion of the purchase price is treated as a charitable gift and the sale portion as a taxable sale.

Partial interest: You cannot generally obtain a deduction for donating a portion of an asset (partial interest) unless you use prescribed techniques such as a charitable remainder trust (CRT), charitable lead trust (CLT), or a remainder interest in a residence or farm. In some instances, less than all of an asset or ownership right may be contributed to charity. There are restrictions on such contributions, so they must be planned to secure a tax deduction.

Partnership: If your partnership donates property, you, as the partner, will report the charitable contribution deduction.

Phaseout: Itemized deductions (expenses you may deduct on your tax return) are subject to certain phaseout rules that may limit those deductions, including charitable contributions.

Present value: The value in current dollars of a sum to be received at some future date or a series of payments to be received over future periods.

Private foundation: You can form your own charity in order to maintain greater control over donations and achieve other personal and family benefits.

Property: You can donate almost any type of property to charity. Each different asset you donate raises its own planning opportunities and issues.

Qualified terminable interest property (QTIP) trust: A trust that qualifies for the unlimited gift and estate tax marital deduction.

Real estate: You can donate real estate to charity directly or to a charitable remainder trust (CRT) to ultimately benefit a named charity. Real estate donations, however, raise a host of issues: mortgages, environmental, title, etc.

Recapture: On the sale or donation of an asset that was depreciated, a portion or all of that depreciation may reduce the charitable contribution deduction.

Remainder interest: The value of property at a future date, after current rights held by another. For example, a donor's spouse can be given the right to income from a trust, and on the spouse's death, a charity may receive any assets left in the trust. The charity's interest is a remainder interest.

Residence: You can donate a remainder interest in your home to charity. You can continue to reside in your home for your life (and your spouse's life, if applicable), and on death, the named charity receives your home. You can qualify for a current income tax deduction for a portion of the value of your home.

Retirement plan: You can bequeath your retirement plan to charity or your retirement assets to satisfy a bequest in your will and save income and estate taxes.

S corporation: S corporation stock can be donated to charity directly or through a charitable remainder trust (CRT). S corporations can donate inventory to charity or deduct certain contributions as advertising expenses.

Spouse: You can combine charitable and marital planning to benefit your spouse and charity and avoid any gift or estate taxes.

Stock: You can donate stock to charity and receive a current income tax deduction. You can use stock to fund various types of trusts to benefit charity.

Substantiation: Donations to charity must be documented in order to secure your tax benefits.

Testamentary: A charitable gift can be made in your will and is effective on your death. This is a testamentary gift.

Wealth-replacement trust: You can donate assets to charity or to a CRT to benefit the organization and form an insurance trust (ILIT) to own insurance on your life to replace the value of the assets donated to charity.

INDEX